LANDMARK VIS

G000037604

New Forest

Gerald Ponting

ABOUT THE AUTHOR

Gerald Ponting is a registered Blue Badge Tourist Guide for Hampshire, Wiltshire and Dorset. He is a keen photographer and is well-known as a speaker at many local societies. Working with colleagues, he has written twelve books concerning the history of several Hampshire communities.

Gerald was brought up in a village on the edge of the New Forest. He was a Biology Teacher for 30 years, taking early retirement in 1992. He spent ten years of his life in the Outer Hebrides. In 1978 he was presented with a British Archaeological Award for studies of the Standing Stones of Callanish, Isle of Lewis.

ACKNOWLEDGEMENTS

The author wishes to thank the following for information, advice and proof-reading – Peter Bennett, Barbara Burbridge, Bridget Hall (Forestry Commission), Barbara Hillier, Anthony Light, Philippa Newnham, Sara St George (New Forest District Council Leisure Services) and Sue Westwood (Verderers' clerk); also the staff of many of the attractions detailed; and fellow members of Viewfinders of Romsey Camera Club for the loan of photographs.

Landmark Publishing thanks Michael Bell of Bells Bookshop, Halifax, Yorkshire (01422) 365468 for supplying the material upon which the maps in this book are based.

THE NEW FOREST

DEDICATION

To the memory of my parents, Ernest and Nellie Ponting,
who loved the Forest in all its moods.

Opposite: Great spotted woodpecker

LANDMARK VISITORS GUIDE

New Forest

Gerald Ponting

· CONTENTS ·

*Many paths lead into the
woodlands*

CARING
FOR THE FOREST

It is hoped that most visitors to the New Forest will be aware of and will observe the Country Code, summarised in the adage 'take nothing but photographs, leave nothing but footprints' (although even footprints can be damaging in some habitats!). The Forest, however, is a very special place so it has its own more extensive code of advice for visitors.

- **Stay below 40mph (64kph) on unfenced roads**
  This greatly reduces the number of accidents affecting ponies, cattle and deer, especially at night. Take the greatest care when passing animals, as *they do not understand cars* and may make unpredictable movements.

- **Use the New Forest car parks**
  There are around 120 of them, so there is no need to cause congestion and damage to verges by parking on the roadside. It is, of course, advisable to lock your car and not to leave valuable items in it.

- **Admire the ponies and donkeys, but do not feed them**
  Animals soon associate cars and people with food. This attracts them to the roadside where they are in danger; some may become aggressive towards visitors when no snack is forthcoming! If a pony lays its ears back alongside its head, back away promptly – this is a threatening posture. Never come between a mare and her foal, as she will see this as a threat and react accordingly.

- **You may walk on any track or footpath in the Forest –**
  unless there is a notice telling you otherwise. Keeping to paths greatly reduces disturbance to wildlife habitats. On Ordnance Survey maps of the Forest, double dashed lines generally indicate a wide, often gravel, track; a single dashed line indicates any other track or footpath.

- **Cycling is permitted on waymarked routes only**
  Cyclists must not use other tracks, paths or open heathland. Wheel-spins and skidding in particular cause erosion. Cyclists should give way to horse-riders and walkers.

- **Fire is a real threat to Forest habitats and wildlife**
  The making of any kind of camp-fire is prohibited. Barbecue sites are provided at two car parks.

- **Keep your dog under control at all times**
  Dogs can cause considerable trouble both for wildlife and for grazing animals. Dogs *must* be kept on a lead in inclosures.

- **Litter is unsightly and can kill animals**
  Take it home with you or put it into the bins provided.

FOREST BYE-LAWS

These are listed on panels at every car park. They include a prohibition on any picking or gathering of plant material. However, collecting fungi is permitted – for personal consumption only. Of course, no-one should consume wild fungi unless they are capable of positively distinguishing between palatable and poisonous species! Specific banning notices are displayed in some woods to help conserve the important fungi populations.

Welcome to the
New Forest

INTRODUCTION

There is nowhere else quite like the New Forest. It is the biggest area of largely unspoilt countryside in the lowlands of southern Britain and one of the few medieval forests remaining in Europe. Against all the odds, an ancient landscape of majestic woodlands, gorse-covered heathland and boggy valleys has survived into the twenty-first century.

> (The) 'intermixture of wood and pasturage, with large separations of heath, give a variety to the forest, which a boundless continuance of woody scenery could not exhibit.'
> *Remarks on Forest Scenery* by William Gilpin (Vicar of Boldre), 1791

Waterlilies at Eyeworth Pond, near Fritham

William the Conqueror set this area apart for the 'beasts of the forest'. Wild boar disappeared long ago but red, roe and fallow deer still live in the woods. Ponies and cattle belonging to the commoners also graze in the open Forest. They prevent the growth of scrub and have been called the 'architects of the Forest landscape'.

The right of pasture was first granted to the common people as compensation for the imposition of

Forest Law. Harsh penalties were inflicted on anyone who harmed the deer or otherwise interfered with the King's pleasure in the hunt. The Crown still owns much of the Forest, managed today with nature conservation and amenity taking precedence over timber production.

The woods and heaths, the small farms, villages and estates, the bogs, ponds and streams together form a complex mosaic of habitats, each one with its own distinctive wildlife. However, the whole is greater than the sum of its parts, making the New Forest an area of the greatest international importance biologically.

Today, the New Forest is many things to many people. To the commoners and foresters it is a way of life as well as a livelihood. To botanists, entomologists, bird-watchers and the like, it has one of the best range of habitats in Britain and must be carefully protected. For many commuters, it provides an opportunity to live in the depths of the countryside while working in the surrounding urban areas.

While visitors are always welcome, there have to be some restrictions if the Forest is to survive the pressures caused by visitor numbers (*see* 'Caring for the Forest'). Golfers, anglers, horse-riders, model-boat enthusiasts and many others are catered for, in one part of the Forest or another. Management of the Forest often involves resolving apparently conflicting interests.

Leave the car & explore!

While this book is arranged in the conventional fashion of tours by road, it is hoped that many visitors will avoid overuse of the car. All touring motorists should leave the car behind as often as possible; that is the only way to really get to know the Forest. Arrive by rail or coach and most parts of the Forest can be explored by a combination of walking, cycling and public transport.

However, I have not seen it as the purpose of this book to give detailed instructions for individual walks or cycle rides. There are several other books and maps which fulfil this function admirably. Any one of them would prove a valuable supplement to this book. In addition, the OS Outdoor Leisure map of the New Forest becomes essential if the visitor intends to penetrate into the heart of the woodlands. Here peace and tranquillity can always be found, even on summer weekends when the car parks are overflowing.

New Forest car parks are often sited among the trees

THE HISTORY OF THE NEW FOREST

The area now occupied by the New Forest would have been relatively unattractive for settlement in prehistoric times; the soil is mostly poor, due to the sands, clay and gravels which make up the local geology. Around 3,000 years ago, though, Bronze Age people cleared woodland to grow crops. Their farming techniques resulted in soil deterioration, thus producing the extensive heathland. The tribes buried their dead in round barrows, of which around 200 are known in the Forest.

Iron Age people constructed a number of hillforts, of which the best preserved today is Buckland Rings at Lymington. In Roman times indigenous resources were used to produce a distinctive type of pottery. Local clay was fired in kilns using the ample supply of firewood. The resulting 'New Forest ware' was distributed throughout southern England.

Our knowledge of the Forest in the 'Dark Ages', the period between about 410AD and 1066, is sparse. However, most of the main settlements known in the Forest area today must have been established by the Saxon period – they are mentioned in Domesday Book and their place-names have Anglo-Saxon origins.

Creation of the Forest

It was around 1079 that William the Conqueror ordered the creation of a new hunting reserve in the area previously known as Ytene. The new name was first recorded in 1086 as Nova Foresta, 'New Forest', in Domesday Book. At that time, a 'forest' was an area of countryside, not necessarily woodland, set aside for the royal beasts of the chase. This provided both sport and meat for the king and his retinue.

The New Forest was considerably bigger then, its perambulation (or boundary) surrounding an area stretching from the Solent almost to Salisbury and from the Avon valley to Southampton Water. It has often

Young calf & mother in snow

been stated that William displaced whole communities to create the Forest, but in fact the area was very sparsely populated to begin with.

The Forest Law

The local inhabitants became subject to the harsh Forest Law, administered by the Verderers' Court. The penalties for poaching the king's deer were death or mutilation. Cutting vegetation which gave food and shelter for the deer was prohibited. No Forest land could be enclosed, so the local people were permitted to graze their ponies, cattle and pigs on the open land. However, the animals had to be taken back to the peasants' tiny holdings in winter, when the scant grazing was reserved for the deer, and also during the 'fence month'. This was the period around midsummer's day when most of the young deer were born.

In 1217, the 'Charter of the Forest' relaxed the Forest Law. The harsher penalties were abandoned and people were allowed, on suitable payment, to enlarge their holdings by fencing more land.

Timber for ships

Wood was, of course, a primary raw material in the Middle Ages. Gradually, the production of timber became more important than the protection of deer, resulting in the first-ever parliamentary Act on tree-protection being passed as early as 1483.

The earliest record of oak from the New Forest being used to build naval ships dates from 1611. A large warship required the timber from at least sixty trees, each around 200 years old. With the demand for vessels to protect England's coasts, it is hardly surprising that, in 1698, Parliament passed an 'Act for the Increase and Preservation of Timber in the New Forest'.

Left: Grey squirrel

Below: The leaves of sundew have sticky hairs to trap insects

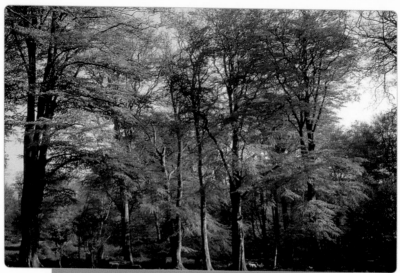

Ancient & Ornamental woodland in the autumn, with the beeches at their best

This instituted the 'rolling power of inclosure'. Up to 6,000 acres (2,430 hectares) of the Forest could be fenced at any one time, to grow timber for naval ship-building. Once young trees had grown too large to be affected by grazing animals, the fences could be removed and the woodland opened for grazing. Then another area up to the same acreage could be enclosed and planted. The Act also banned the practice of pollarding – the cutting of branches for animal feed.

Disputes between Crown and Commoners

The last king to use his right to hunt in the Forest was James II in the 1680s. Deer were soon seen as a hindrance to efficient timber production, as fences were no obstacle to them; they ate tree seedlings, thus preventing regeneration. Eventually, this led to the 'New Forest Deer Removal Act' of 1851. The plan to eliminate all the deer inevitably failed, but numbers fell considerably.

The Act contained other sweeping changes. The maximum area of 'rolling inclosure' was greatly increased. Within the first year, 4,000 acres (1,620 hectares) were planted, mostly with conifers. All commoners' rights had to be registered by a new committee – which systematically refused many applications and reduced the value of others. As a result, the number of commoners declined, as did the amount of grazing available to their animals.

Commoners' Charter

Like that of 1698, the 1851 Act resulted in conflict between the Crown's interest in timber production and the commoners' interest in grazing. The problems were largely resolved by the New Forest Act of 1877, sometimes called the 'Commoners' Charter'. The Verderers' Court was re-established with a totally different role – to protect the rights of the commoners. The rolling power of inclosure was ended. The more ancient woods were to be left unenclosed, so that animals could graze in them.

Pony & Scots pine on heathland, Pig Bush near Beaulieu

Changes in the twentieth century

During and between World War I and II, many trees were felled and large areas were planted with conifers. In 1923, the Crown lands became the responsibility of the new Forestry Commission.

In the second half of the twentieth century measures were taken to improve conditions for visitors, while reducing their environmental impact; to put wildlife conservation much nearer the top of the 'Forest agenda'; and to reduce the risks of animals being killed or injured by traffic.

In the early 1960s, cattle grids were installed where roads crossed the Forest perambulation – previously, ponies had often strayed outside, sometimes raiding gardens! At around the same time the A31 trunk road was fenced to reduce accidents involving animals – soon followed by the fencing of the A35 and A337. All other roads through the New Forest remain unfenced, but with a blanket speed limit of 40mph (64kph) introduced in the 1990s.

In the 1960s and 1970s, the impact of visitors and their cars, tents and caravans was having a disastrous effect on the Forest. At that time, there was nothing to prevent motorists driving onto the open Forest and parking wherever their vehicles could take them. The answer was to provide many carefully-sited car parks, with ditches and barriers to make most of the Forest car-free. By 1976 this had been completed, along with the establishment of official camping sites.

Wildlife conservation

The Act passed in 1877 recognised the amenity value of the unfenced and grazed woodlands, giving them a grand title which is still used – 'The Ancient and Ornamental Woodlands'. Today, they are managed for conservation and amenity, not for timber production.

The Forest's 'important nature reserve status' was accepted by the

Forestry Commission as early as 1949. In 1971 the entire New Forest was declared a Site of Special Scientific Interest. English Nature now takes a major role in many decisions concerning the management of the Forest.

The biological importance of the Forest has been recognised internationally by the provision of EU funds for the LIFE Project, which commenced in 1997. The purpose is to preserve and enhance biodiversity by removing scrub, repairing erosion, restoring damaged wetlands and the like.

New Forest Heritage Area, which was defined at the same time.

The Heritage Area extends beyond the perambulation in order to reduce the possibility that new developments just outside the Forest proper would have harmful effects within it.

The Countryside Agency is drawing up plans to institute the New Forest National Park with extended boundaries. It remains to be seen what the relationship will be between a new National Park Authority and existing organisations.

Heritage Area and National Park

In 1990 the New Forest Committee was set up, providing for closer consultation between the Forestry Commission, the Verderers, English Nature, local farmers and landowners, the county and district councils, and the Environment and Countryside Agencies. Its aim is to protect and enhance the special nature of the

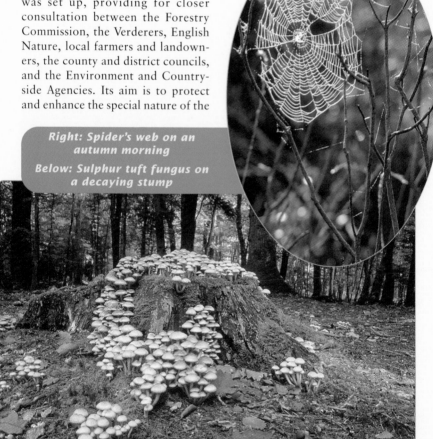

Right: Spider's web on an autumn morning

Below: Sulphur tuft fungus on a decaying stump

HABITATS AND LANDSCAPES OF THE NEW FOREST

Almost any walk in the Forest will take the visitor through several different habitats, with the chance of seeing a variety of wildlife. This section can be no more than a brief summary of the various habitats.

The Ancient and Ornamental Woodlands

As early as 1877, Parliament recognised the need to preserve the 'picturesque character' of these unfenced woodlands, where domestic stock can wander at will. 'Pasture woodland' is a very unusual habitat, even on a European scale.

Deep in an area of A&O Woodland, the visitor is transported back to a landscape from medieval England. One would hardly be surprised to see a Norman king and his retinue pursuing their quarry through one of the open glades! The deer themselves are most likely to be seen early or late in the day.

Oak and beech dominate in the A&O Woods, often with a shrub layer of holly and sometimes hawthorn. While the woods are attractive at any time of year, the beeches in particular become a riot of brown, yellow, gold and russet in the late autumn. A vast range of fungus species appears at this time of year; ferns, mosses and lichens are also common.

As trees are allowed to live out their natural life-span and fallen trees are cleared only if they obstruct paths and tracks, there is plenty of old, dead and decaying timber. This provides homes for beetles and other insects, which in turn become food for a variety of birds. Woodpeckers, treecreepers and nuthatches are

Deer

The commonest species is the fallow deer, with up to 1,000 in the Forest. Their coat is dark in the winter, but chestnut with white spots in the summer. About a hundred of the much larger red deer frequent the woods and heathlands, with a small semi-domesticated herd at Burley. Around sixty sika deer, a Japanese species, live mainly in woods to the east of Brockenhurst. The small roe deer are sometimes seen by those who make a point of walking quietly in the woods; there are about 300 of them. The muntjac, another 'foreign invader', is tiny and very rarely seen.

NEW FOREST BADGER WATCH

Weather-proof hide with view of active badger sett both above and below ground; commentary on headphones. No children under 7; no still cameras. Limited capacity, book well ahead. Meeting point and time notified on booking. Visits lasting one hour every evening March-October. Prior booking by phone essential, call between 9-10am only, 1st Feb-31st Oct. ☎ 01425 403412

common, along with many other species of woodland birds and predators like owls and hawks. Badgers are also common but rarely seen by the casual visitor.

Hardwood inclosures

Inclosures are planted woodlands, fenced to keep out domestic livestock. In the days before fencing, they were enclosed by earth banks, topped with dense plantings of thorny shrubs. Traces of these banks remain in many places in the Forest. Before 1851, species planted were mainly oak with some beech and sweet chestnut.

Grassy tracks through the woodland, known as rides, are the best areas for wild flowers, especially in the spring. Dog violets and the yellowish-green heads of wood spurge are particularly common. Oak, bramble, honeysuckle, ivy and even some grasses are the food plants of numerous butterflies – meadow browns, various skippers and fritillaries, commas and so on.

Coniferous inclosures

Conifers became the norm for forestry plantation after the 1851 Act, but few have been planted since 1977. Most are not native British species, Norway spruce, Corsican pine and Douglas fir having been chosen by the Forestry Commission for their speed of growth, becoming mature in as little as fifty years.

Wildlife is generally less numerous in coniferous woodland than in hardwood areas. However, some birds such as siskins, crossbills and redpolls, and some fungi, prefer this habitat. Tall heaps of pine needles under the trees are the nests of wood ants.

In any of the woodlands, the most frequently seen mammal is the grey squirrel. This introduced North American species is not generally welcomed by foresters, as it strips the bark from young trees.

Open heathland

Some areas of heathland are dominated by one or more of the three species of heather found in the Forest. Others are mainly composed of rough grasses. The dominant vegetation is often broken up by stands of bracken and clumps of gorse bushes. Gorse, known locally as 'furze', produces masses of brilliant yellow pea-flowers mainly in the spring and early summer. But there are some flowers on the gorse, whatever the time of year. As the local saying goes:

'When furze is not in bloom
Kissing is out of season !'

Many people are surprised to see ponies and donkeys nibbling happily

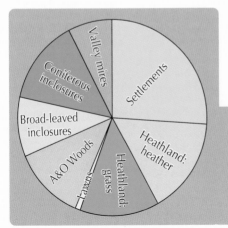

Above: Gorse in bloom on Furzley Common, Bramshaw

Left: Foraging pigs disturb the ground in their search for tasty roots

on the prickly gorse. Both gorse and heather are deliberately burnt in patches on a regular cycle, ensuring that there is always a supply of fresh young shoots which are more palatable than old ones.

Trees growing on the heathland include Scots pine, which was first planted in the Forest in 1776 and now seeds itself; rowan or mountain ash; crab apple, and silver birch.

Flowers include the tiny yellow tormentil, purple lousewort and a variety of orchids. Some are found only in limited areas, but the small heath spotted orchid is commonly seen. The greatest floral treasure of the New Forest is the carefully protected wild gladiolus, which grows nowhere else in Britain. It is rarely seen by the casual visitor, flowering

Valley mires

Coniferous inclosures

Settlements

Broad-leaved inclosures

Heathland: heather

A&O Woods

Lawns

Heathland: grass

This diagram shows the approximate proportion of the different habitats within the Forest perambulation. This covers an area of 145 square miles (375 sq km). The New Forest Heritage Area covers 224 square miles (581 sq km)

in early summer under fronds of bracken.

The most distinctive bird of the heathland is the Dartford warbler, which is uncommon in other parts of the country. Stonechats are common, while linnets and a number of woodland species nest in gorse thickets.

The Forest is home to all six British species of reptile – adder, grass snake, slow-worm, common lizard, as well as the rare smooth snake and sand lizard. The presence of the adder, Britain's only poisonous snake, alarms some visitors. But an adder is very sensitive to vibration and will normally move away long before footfalls reach the spot where it is sunning itself. However, in spring, when they have just emerged from hibernation, they may be too sluggish to move out of the way. This is another good reason to stay on paths and not to tramp through vegetation.

Forest lawns

A 'lawn' in the New Forest is not a patch carefully tended with a lawnmower! – but an area of grass kept short by the numbers of ponies and cattle which regularly graze on it. Most lawns are quite natural, but a number result from deliberate re-seeding in the 1940s and 1950s, in some cases on former World War II airfields.

Though the lawns form only a small proportion of the overall area of open land, they are extremely important, especially those alongside streams, as they provide the best grazing in the Forest. Plants other than grasses are limited to those resistant to grazing pressure, including daisies, plantains and clover.

Valley mires

The valley mires of the New Forest, 'bogs' to most people, may be

Many New Forest thatched cottages are now highly desirable residences

unattractive to walkers and some-times dangerous for livestock, but in terms of biological diversity they are of incalculable value. There are around ninety separate mires, un-spoilt by drainage or any form of 'land reclamation', within the Forest. They probably represent well over half of all such habitats in the whole of Europe!

The plants of the mires are best observed where road bridges or foot-bridges cross the swampy land. The low bushy bog myrtle is common, as is the 'bog-moss', *Sphagnum*. Perhaps the most fascinating of the bog plants are the different species of the insect-ivorous sundew. They compensate for the lack of nutrients in the damp peaty soil by using sticky hairs on their leaves to catch insects, which they digest. Nearby, the yellow bog asphodel often grows. The boggy land alongside some streams supports a dense growth of alder trees.

Siskins and redpolls feed on the seeds of the alder, while the insect life of the mires includes several species of dragonflies and their more slender relatives, the damselflies.

Streams and ponds

The largest of the streams which flow through the Forest are the Lymington River and the Beaulieu River. Other smaller watercourses go by such delightful names as Dockens Water and King's Garn Gutter.

In a few places, the water flow is slow and muddy stream beds have developed, allowing water plants to grow. But in most places the beds are gravelly and the flow quite strong, especially after rain, so few plants can live in the streams. Fishes such as minnows, sticklebacks and even trout thrive; they attract kingfishers,

which nest in holes in the stream banks, and herons, which have a heronry at Sowley Pond.

This pond is the largest in the Forest but is on private land. Other relatively large ponds include Hatchet Pond and Eyeworth. There are many smaller ponds, some cre-ated especially to provide water for commoners' stock.

Mallards, teal and other water-birds, damselflies and dragonflies, frogs, toads and newts all frequent the ponds in varying numbers.

The coastal fringe

The Forest perambulation meets the waters of the Solent between the mouths of the Lymington and Beaulieu Rivers. Much of the coast-line, however, is occupied by private land-holdings. The mud-flats and salt-marshes, with their distinctive saline-tolerant flora and numerous sea-birds and waders, are better appreciated on the nature reserves and public paths to the west of Lymington.

Farms, estates and villages

About a quarter of the area of the Forest is occupied by villages, farms, smallholdings and private estates, of which the largest is the Beaulieu Estate. Many of the land-holdings, of course, are occupied by the common-ers who own the depastured* stock – which continues to graze on road-side verges and other open spaces within the settlements. The common-ers' holdings with their hedges, pastureland and cultivated fields add one more element to the complex and fascinating mosaic of habitats which make up the New Forest.

* *See* 'Glossary – New Forest Words'

PONIES, COMMONERS AND AGISTERS

For many visitors, the most characteristic feature of the New Forest is the presence of free-ranging ponies. They are encountered on open heathland and lawns, in the depths of the ancient woodlands – and on the roadsides, where they are at risk from careless drivers who ignore the necessary 40mph (64kph) speed limit.

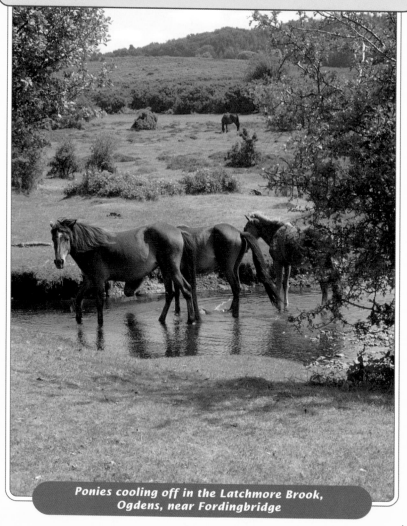

Ponies cooling off in the Latchmore Brook, Ogdens, near Fordingbridge

Not everyone realises at first that the ponies are not 'wild'. Their owners, known as commoners, are all occupiers of holdings to which the Common Right of Pasture is attached. There are about 350 active commoners today with an average of around ten ponies each.

Commoning as a way of life is essential to the survival of the Forest; without the grazing animals the unenclosed habitats would change drastically. Unfortunately, there are many factors acting against commoning, including the general downturn in agricultural income. Few have ever expected to make a complete living from commoning and many commoners have other jobs.

Because of the desire of 'outsiders' to live in the Forest, properties (which incidentally have common rights attached) often command a market price well above that which intending commoners can afford. However, those brought up in the Forest generally feel a very strong incentive to continue in the traditional way of life, while the New Forest Council has policies to encourage the continuation of commoning.

The health of the ponies and other stock – and dealing with those injured or killed on the roads – is the responsibility of the six Agisters, paid officials employed by the Verderers. The Forest is divided into five areas, with an Agister responsible for each, while the Head Agister covers the whole Forest. Each pony has its tail clipped into a pattern which indicates to which area it belongs.

From August to November, the Agisters organise around forty-five 'drifts'. Local commoners, on horseback, round up the ponies in a limited section of the Forest and collect them in a temporary paddock or pound. Each pony is checked and dosed against worms. Some, at their owners' request, are fitted with reflective collars to reduce the risk of night-time road accidents.

Young foals are branded with their owner's mark, and each animal is tail-marked. The fee, which each commoner pays to the Verderers to depasture the pony, is known as the 'marking fee'. Once all of this has been done, many of the ponies are released. The rest are taken away by their owners in horse-boxes, perhaps destined for the next Pony Sale on the heathland near Beaulieu Road Station. All young colts are removed from the open Forest, as, in order to maintain the quality of the New Forest breed, only registered stallions are allowed to breed with the mares.

New Forest Ponies

The New Forest pony is a hardy breed and most of them remain on the open forest all winter, using gorse and woodland for shelter in the worst weather. Each group of ponies tends to have its own distinct area, and rarely wanders outside it. In the heat of summer, mixed herds of ponies, cattle and sometimes donkeys gather together in particular spots, known as 'shades'. Ironically, these often have no shade from the sun. It is believed that the stock are less troubled by biting insects in these areas. The position of a shade remains established over many generations – and some overlap modern motor-roads.

KEEPERS, FORESTERS AND RANGERS

The post of Keeper goes back to the time of the Norman kings. The Forest was then divided into 'walks', with one keeper responsible for the royal deer in each walk. Today, there are twelve sections, called beats, and the keepers are employed by the Forestry Commission. Each keeper lives in a cottage within his beat, often deep in the woods – and he is still responsible for the deer in his area.

With no natural predators in the Forest today, deer numbers have to be controlled or they would soon outstrip the food supply. Each spring's cull is carefully planned to maintain a balance of ages and sexes within the population. Thus the keepers, who carry out the cull, have to be expert shots. A keeper is knowledgeable, not just about the deer, but about all the wildlife in his beat. Keepers work with the foresters to ensure that forestry operations do not interfere with the interests of wildlife.

Over one hundred people are employed in commercial forestry. Conifers are the most important crop, with only about ten per cent of the timber being hardwood from broad-leaved trees. It takes fifty to sixty years before young conifers are ready for felling, although some wood is produced when twenty-year-old plantations are thinned. On each working day through the year, the foresters produce the equivalent of eight lorry-loads of wood. Timber from the Forest is used mainly in building and fencing, while twenty-five per cent becomes paper pulp or chipboard.

The ranger service was introduced in the early 1990s as the 'public face' of the Forestry Commission. The six rangers run a programme of walks and other events for the public (*see* 'Guided Walks' in the FactFile). They are also responsible for recreational activities, introducing school groups to the Forest and other educational ventures.

When a partly mature plantation is thinned, the timber is stacked alongside the rides, awaiting transport

COMMON RIGHTS

Common rights have existed as long as the Forest and are linked not to individuals but to land holdings. There are six distinct rights, recorded on definitive maps drawn up in the 1950s.

THE RIGHT OF COMMON PASTURE

This is the most important of the common rights, both for the commoners and for the maintenance of the Forest environment. Without the cattle and ponies which graze in the New Forest, heathland would turn to scrub and scrub to woodland. Animal numbers fluctuate over the years, but in 1999 there were around 2,300 cattle, 3,400 ponies and 70 donkeys depastured in the Forest.

THE COMMON PASTURE OF SHEEP

Sheep are sometimes seen in the Forest, as a few holdings have the right to graze them, mainly around Bramshaw and Godshill.

THE RIGHT OF COMMON MAST

Mast refers not just to beech-nuts, but also to unripe acorns which fall in great numbers in the autumn. If cattle or ponies eat too many, it can make them ill. But pigs love them and thrive on them. So, for sixty or more days each year, the pannage season, around a hundred pigs roam the Forest. They are most frequently seen on the Bramshaw Commons, where the right exists throughout the year.

THE RIGHT TO FUELWOOD OR ESTOVERS

At one time, the collection of wood for fuel was essential for most Forest dwellers. Only around 70 holdings still retain the ancient right of Estovers, and their firewood is now cut for them by the Forestry Commission, the commoners having to arrange collection.

This inn-sign at East Boldre commemorates the ancient Common Right of Turbary

The Right to Common Marl

This right, which is no longer used, was to extract limy clay from pits in the Forest. Before the use of fertilisers, clay was used to improve sandy soils in cultivated areas. It was also an ingredient of cob, once an important building material.

The Right of Turbary

The right to cut 'turf' (or peat) for use as fuel is no longer practised.

Above: Bracken

Below: Bell heather

Bracken and Heather

Though not formal rights, many commoners once cut bracken and heather, practices which have almost died out. The heather was used for thatching outbuildings and even under the main thatch of cottages. The bracken, locally known as 'fern', made excellent animal bedding. Today the Forestry Commission keeps this invasive plant under control by cutting for compost; it makes an excellent peat substitute for gardeners.

LYNDHURST

All visitors to the Forest should spend some time in Lyndhurst, if only to visit the New Forest Museum. The village also caters for many other needs, with shops supplying books, maps, provisions, camping equipment, and many types of gifts and souvenirs. There is also a wide range of tea-rooms, pubs and restaurants.

Although a village, Lyndhurst has always been considered the 'capital of the New Forest'. At the time of the Domesday Book (1086), when the name was spelt 'Linhest', it was in the hands of the king. It is here that the New Forest District Council and the Verderers' Court both meet and where the Forestry Commission has its local offices.

NEW FOREST MUSEUM AND VISITOR CENTRE

Lyndhurst central car park
Museum of New Forest history and traditions; gift shop with local crafts; full wheelchair access; Resource Centre; Visitor Information Centre in same building. Open: daily from 10am.
☎ 023 8028 3914

The **New Forest Museum** tells the story of the Forest through a seventeen-minute audio-visual show and a series of well-arranged displays and dioramas. As well as local history and traditions, it also deals with local characters, habitats and wildlife, the commoning way of life and forestry management, all in a manner which attracts children as well as informing adults.

A special feature is the New Forest Embroidery, created in 1979 to commemorate the nine hundredth anniversary of the New Forest. The concept was inspired by the Bayeux Tapestry and covers all the main historical events over nine hundred years, also illustrating the Forest's flora and fauna.

Victorian church

The **Parish Church of St Michael and All Angels** is an imposing Victorian brick structure dating from the 1860s. The fine east window contains stained glass considered *'infinitely superior to anything done by anyone else at that time'* (Pevsner, *'The Buildings of England – Hampshire'*). It was the work of Edward Burne-Jones and William Morris; the church has several other links with the pre-Raphaelite school of artists.

Behind the altar is a fresco of the 'Wise and Foolish Virgins' by Lord Leighton. When he painted this in 1862, he charged only for the cost of his materials, as he was trying out a new method of wall-painting intended to survive English weather conditions. It is said that local 'ladies' were the models for the wise virgins and poorer women posed as the foolish virgins!

Alice in Wonderland

On the south side of the churchyard is the simple tomb of the local Hargreaves family, much visited as the **'tomb of Alice in Wonderland'**. Alice Liddell of Oxford, the inspiration for Lewis Carroll's Alice, married Reginald Hargreaves and lived much of her life at Cuffnells House, Lyndhurst. A memorial inside the church commemorates two of her sons killed in the first World War.

Queen's House

Not far from the parish church is **Queen's House**, always known as King's House when a king is on the throne. This was formerly the residence of the Lord Warden of the Forest, but now houses the offices of the Forestry Commission, with the ancient Verderers' Hall at one end. Part of the building dates from as early as the fourteenth century, but much of what we see today was added at the time of the Stuart monarchs.

The arched doorway, facing the road at the eastern end of Queen's House, is the entrance to the courtroom used ten times a year for open sessions of the Verderers' Court, which is not otherwise open to the public. (See pages 36/37.)

Bolton's Bench and Swan Green

One of Lyndhurst's two cricket pitches, near the Beaulieu road, has a thatched pavilion. It is overlooked by **Bolton's Bench**, a hillock crowned with a distinctive growth of yew, with seats beneath. It was named after Lord Bolton, Lord Warden of the Forest in 1688.

At the other end of the village, by the Christchurch road, the second cricket pitch is on **Swan Green**. Named from the Swan Inn which it overlooks, this is one of the most picturesque village scenes in Hampshire. Photographs of the immaculate thatched cottages adjacent to the green must have featured on many postcards and biscuit tins!

With five traffic routes meeting at Lyndhurst, the approaches to the village often have long traffic queues at peak times, despite a one-way circulation. (As any route for a by-pass would involve damage to New Forest habitats, all proposals have been rejected.) The next section considers a number of short excursions, radiating out from Lyndhurst. They could be undertaken on bicycles, perhaps hired from **AA Bike Hire** in Gosport Lane, though fast motor roads are included in some routes.

AROUND LYNDHURST

There are extensive areas of woodland to the south of Lyndhurst, which are easily reached from Clayhill car park on the east of the A337 Brockenhurst road, and Whitley Wood car park (no dogs) on the west. On the same road, almost 3 miles (2km) from the village, is the entrance to New Park. This is home to the largest annual event in the area, the New Forest Show.

Cricket on Swan Green, Lyndhurst

A short distance from Swan Green is the hamlet of **Emery Down** and the New Forest Inn, a popular pub with an interesting history. Ale was originally sold here, around 200 years ago, from a caravan. Extensions were added till it became a permanent building, with part of the original caravan structure still at the heart of it today!

Taking the left turn by the pub, a minor road leads through woodland and after 3 miles (5km), reaches Bolderwood car park (see Ringwood chapter). On the way, shortly after **Millyford Bridge car park**, there is a strange structure, set a little way back on the left of the road. This is the 'Portuguese Fireplace'.

During World War I a detachment of the Portuguese Army worked as lumberjacks in this area, cutting timber which was transported across the channel for building trenches, huts

NEW FOREST AND HAMPSHIRE COUNTY SHOW

Follow special traffic signs from Lyndhurst or Brockenhurst

Many horse events, rings for cattle and sheep, flower show, dog show, hundreds of trade stands, craft show, exhibits by Forestry Commission and other organisations, etc. Phone local VICs for more details. Generally on the last Tuesday, Wednesday and Thursday of July. Ring events from 8am each day.

and walkways. The fireplace was the only stone structure in their hutted camp and remained as a memorial after the rest was demolished.

Minstead

Taking the A337 road north out of Lyndhurst, a left turning after $1\frac{1}{4}$ miles (2km) leads to the scattered village of **Minstead**. The pub and the church are both near the small central green, and both are of interest.

The pub is **The Trusty Servant**; its sign is a copy of an original painting in Winchester College dating from around 1600. According to the artist, the qualities of an ideal servant would be: the body of a pig (which will eat anything), the feet of a stag (for swiftness) and the ears of a donkey (for patience). The pig's snout is locked for secrecy and the creature holds the tools of his trade, a shovel, a brush and a pitch-fork.

All Saints' Church has a rather strange shape, the south transept

being longer than the nave! The Georgian-style interior furnishings are unusual, with box pews and galleries, the highest of which, reserved for the poor, was known as the 'gypsies' gallery'. The pew once reserved for the owners of Castle Malwood house has its own fireplace! There is also a three-tier pulpit; box pews meant that the preacher had to be high up in order to be seen. The

Conan Doyle

Sherlock Holmes aficionados will be interested in a tombstone under an oak tree at the southern end of the churchyard. Sir Arthur Conan Doyle died in Sussex in 1930 and was later re-buried here, near his former home at Bignell House, Minstead. His book *'The White Company'* (1891) is largely set in and around the Forest.

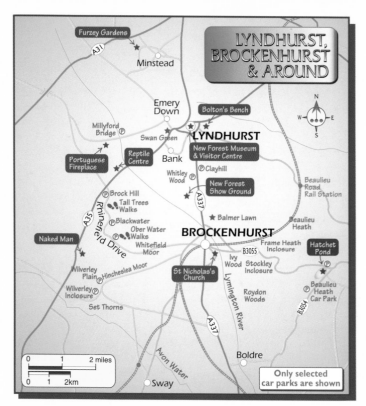

second tier was used by lay-readers and the lowest tier by the clerk.

Near the south-west end of the church is the intriguing tomb of Thomas Maynard, who died in 1807. It bears a carving of the old wind instrument known as a serpent; Thomas had probably played in one of the church bands, which were common before the introduction of organs.

Just to the east of the main path is the memorial stone for Thomas White, initially described as a 'faithful husband'. But his widow began to hear stories and had the word 'faithful' removed – leaving a very obvious rectangular space on the stone!

Furzey Gardens

A short distance away, around Minstead's network of lanes, is **Furzey Gardens**. It is connected with a charity that provides horticultural training for young people with learning disabilities, and plants grown by the students are on sale in the nursery shop.

There is botanical interest here all the year round, with a lake, a fernery, a heather garden, rhododendrons and azaleas, as well as Chilean fire trees and a 'bottle-brush tree'.

There are two thatched buildings within the cottage-style gardens. **Forest Cottage** is believed to be well over 400 years old. Visitors can wander in and admire the open hearth, the bread-oven and other features – an opportunity to obtain a real feel of how life was once lived in the Forest. Nearby is the **Will Selwood Art and Craft Gallery**.

New Forest Reptile Centre

Three miles (2km) from Lyndhurst on the A35 Christchurch road, a gravel track leads off to the right. The **Reptile Centre** at Holidays Hill is a free facility provided by the Forestry Commission to give visitors a chance to see some of the more elusive wildlife of the Forest. All the species of reptile and amphibian which live in the wild in Britain – snakes, lizards, frogs, toads and newts – are housed here in eight open-air pens.

To the south-west of Lyndhurst, accessible either by Pinkney Lane or from a turning off the Christchurch road about half-way to the Reptile Centre, is the little village of **Bank**, with its popular traditional pub, The Oak. A short walk into the woodlands from here is the very unusual settlement of **Gritnam**. In this hamlet, each cottage has its garden, but there are no fields or paddocks – the whole place is incredibly compact for an ancient settlement.

A story passed down in a local family tells of how a Queen (which Queen was not specified), riding through the Forest, tore her clothing. A Gritnam villager mended it for her and as a reward the Queen gave permission to enclose from the Forest as much land as the family could dig in a specified time. No-one bothered to dig, the permission lapsed and so Gritnam remained the same size!

NEW FOREST REPTILE CENTRE

Holidays Hill, Lyndhurst, off A35, 2 miles (3km) west of Lyndhurst Eight open-air pens in a Forest clearing; display panels; rangers often on hand. Parking fee, no admission charge. Open: daily 10am-4.30pm April-September.
☎ 023 8028 3141

BROCKENHURST AND AROUND

Brockenhurst, 4 miles (6.5km) south of Lyndhurst on the A337, is the largest of the New Forest villages. Within a short distance, there are several Forestry Commission waymarked walks. For visitors not inclined to map-read their way into the depths of the Forest, these walks provide an excellent means of seeing some of the natural habitats.

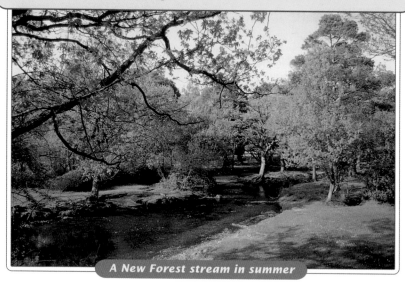

A New Forest stream in summer

Brockenhurst

The name 'Brockenhurst' is traditionally said to mean 'badger's wood'. However, 'broken wooded hill' may be a more likely interpretation – broken in the sense of divided by the valleys of streams. Records say that, in the twelfth century, the Manor was held by Peter Spilman. In return, he had to provide litter for the King's bed and hay for his horse, 'when the king should be at Brockenhurst'.

The main street, Brookley Road, has a reasonable number of specialist shops catering for locals and visitors alike. In spite of cattle grids, ponies sometimes wander through the shopping areas.

By the entrance to one of the two car parks stands a brick plinth. Attached to it is a 'wheel plate', a great disc of cast iron which was used until 1915 by the local forge when applying metal rims to wooden wagon wheels.

It is not unusual for minor roads in the Forest to pass through fords, though most are frequently dry. The most famous is the Brockenhurst 'watersplash' at the western end of Brookley Road. Vehicles leaving the village for Rhinefield or Burley generally have to drive through a few inches of water here.

At the other end of Brookley Road, near the main-line rail station, are the **New Forest Cycle Experience** and three pubs, the Foresters Arms, the Morant Arms and the Snake-catcher. The latter name commemorates a famous local character who died in 1905, aged sixty-seven (see below).

Heading south out of Brockenhurst, there are sometimes traffic delays, due to level-crossing gates near the station. Shortly after, a lane to the left leads to **St Nicholas's Church**, (generally open for visitors between 2.30 and 5pm). The church is the oldest in the Forest and has a fine Norman doorway in the south porch. In the churchyard, near Brusher Mills' grave, there is, surprisingly, a New Zealand war cemetery. Neat rows of tombstones commemorate over one hundred soldiers who died in a nearby field hospital during World War I.

About half a mile (0.8km) southwards, on the Brockenhurst-Lymington road (A337), is the Filly Inn. Just past the inn, down a short lane, a footpath leads to **Roydon Woods Nature Reserve**. While not within the perambulation of the New Forest, the landscape is similar – ancient woodland with some areas of meadow and heath. As grazing

---

ROYDON WOODS NATURE RESERVE

Access from lane off the A337, just south of the Filly Inn

Ancient woodland rich in wildlife with some areas of both dry and wet heathland, keep to public footpaths. Information leaflet from Hampshire Wildlife Trust. Open: at all times.
☎ 023 8061 3636

'Brusher' Mills

The tomb of Harry Mills, better known as **'Brusher' Mills**, is in the graveyard of the parish church, St Nicholas. His nickname came from his practice of brushing Brockenhurst cricket pitch before a match to remove twigs and leaves – and, no doubt, animal droppings. But his main claim to fame was that he made his living by catching snakes in the Forest, apparently immune to the bite of an adder.

He prepared a primitive anti-snakebite serum from the snakes themselves, despatching any spare specimens to London Zoo as food for secretary birds and the like. He was not averse to earning gratuities from visitors by capturing snakes which had suddenly appeared among them – snakes which he had surreptitiously released himself!

A carving on his tombstone shows the wattle and daub hut in which he lived in the depths of the Forest for the last twenty years of his life.

by domestic stock is carefully controlled, the reserve has a wider variety of plant life than many grazed areas in the Forest.

A short distance further along the A337, there is a right turning towards Sway. The first Forest car park on the left is by a pond reserved for the use of model yacht enthusiasts. The road continues across open heathland; a left turning leads to **Sway**.

Sway and Wilverley

The village of Sway is largely of post-railway age, but there are some older corners with thatched cottages. Captain Marryatt's Victorian novel, *'The Children of the New Forest'*, was set in this area. Sway also boasts **Artsway**, an award-winning contemporary art gallery.

ARTSWAY

*Station Road, Sway
near Forest Heath Hotel*
Outdoor sculpture, temporary exhibitions, talks, events and workshops, working artists' studios; full disabled access.
Open: 11am-5pm Tuesday-Sunday. ☎ 01590 682260

---

here – the lawn provides much better grazing than heathland. During World War II, it was ploughed to supplement war-time food production. After the war, no longer needed to produce cereals and potatoes, it was re-seeded with grass and clover. Since then, the grassland has gradually reverted to a state similar to the completely natural lawns.

Wilverley Plain car park has public toilets while the nearby Wilverley Inclosure **car park** has a barbecue site

---

Peterson's Tower

Sway's oddest claim to fame, and one which dominates the view from much of the open heathland nearby, is Sway Tower (situated on private land). Also known as **Peterson's Tower**, it was built in the 1880s by Andrew Peterson, a retired judge from British India. It is 218ft (66.5m) high and took five years to build, with the purpose of demonstrating the value of concrete as a building material. It is said that Peterson, a spiritualist, received architectural directions from none other than Sir Christopher Wren!

The 'Naked Man'

A feature known as the 'Naked Man', marked on OS Maps, is situated near the northern edge of Wilverley Inclosure. It may be approached from Wilverley Plain car park or, as a shorter walk, from Wilverley Post on the A35. There is little to see today – the stump of a tree covered with ivy and protected by a fence. Not so long ago, it was a gaunt dead oak with two projecting branches like arms. Further back in history, when this track was part of the road to Burley, the tree had a sinister use. Smugglers and highwaymen were hanged here as a deterrent to others passing by.

Leaving the village to the north, a minor road runs alongside Set Thorns Inclosure and across heathland towards the level lawn of **Wilverley Plain**. Many animals gather (bookable). A $2^1/_2$-mile (4.2km) waymarked walk through **Wilverley Inclosure**, suitable for accompanied wheelchairs and baby-buggies, may be started from either car park. This is a commercially managed woodland which produces around 1,000 tonnes of timber in a year. Nevertheless, the scene is quite varied, with young and mature conifers interspersed with sweet chestnut, oak and beech.

From Wilverley, a minor road leads directly back to Brockenhurst across **Hincheslea Moor**, where a network of footpaths may be used to explore the undulating heathland. This route returns to the village centre via the watersplash.

Ober Water and Rhinefield

The other road out of Brockenhurst, via the ford, crosses **Whitefield Moor**, which often attracts large numbers of ponies and cattle. Like Wilverley Plain, it was cultivated during World War II, then re-seeded.

Ober Water Walks

At the far end of the lawn is Whitefield Moor car park (toilets). This is the departure point for the **Ober Water Walks**, which give views of woodland, heathland, lawn and stream. There are two routes, one of 1 mile (1.5km) and one of $1^1/_2$ miles (2.5km); they are way-marked in different colours and both are entirely on gravel paths.

Beyond Whitefield Moor, the road enters extensive woodlands. Drivers should take great care here, as there

Rhinefield Walks

The exotic tree species of Rhinefield Drive may be appreciated on the waymarked **Tall Trees Walk** ($1^1/_2$ miles (2.5km) which loops from Blackwater car park (toilets) to Brock Hill car park and back again.

A shorter alternative, the **Blackwater Arboretum Trail** ($^1/_2$ mile (0.75km) and suitable for wheelchairs) passes through an arboretum started in 1960, with specimens of many broad-leaved and coniferous trees. Interpretative panels suggest that visitors 'use their senses to discover the secrets that these trees hold'.

is often little room for two cars to pass. The nearby **Rhinefield House Hotel** was built as a private house in 1887, on the site of a much older Forest keeper's lodge. The gardens are restored to their 1890s design, while the interior features rooms based on Westminster Hall and the Alhambra Palace!

Rhinefield Drive was the private drive of the house until 1938 and had been planted with specimen trees in 1859 when it was fashionable for landowners to experiment with exotic tree species. They include Spanish fir, black spruce, red spruce, Lawson cypress, Weymouth pine, Wellingtonia and western red cedar. Several that have grown to maturity are thought to be the tallest of their kind in Britain.

Balmer Lawn and Hatchet Pond

On the northern outskirts of Brockenhurst, just off the A337 Lyndhurst road, stands the **Balmer Lawn** Hotel. The 'lawn' extends to about 200 acres (81 hectares) to the north and east of the hotel. At one time, New Forest ponies competed on a race-track here! Today, the visitor may explore the nearby inclosures on foot or on a bicycle from **Balmer Lawn Bike Hire**. The car park by the Lymington River is very popular in summer.

Just to the south of the hotel, the B3055 road leads towards Beaulieu. The first Forest car park, Ivy Wood, provides access to an area of oak woodland alongside the Lymington river. The road then passes between several inclosures.

The Brockenhurst-Beaulieu road comes out of the woods onto **Beaulieu Heath** by Stockley Inclosure

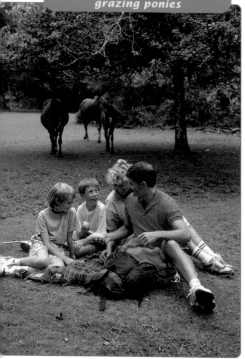

Forest lawns are equally suitable for family picnics and grazing ponies

Hatchet Pond

Hatchet Pond is a very popular spot, providing a scenic backdrop for picnics, plenty of ducks for children to feed and some-times dramatic summer sunsets. The pond was created in the eighteenth century to provide water-power for an iron mill. 'Hatchet' is an old Forest term for a gateway through which ponies and cattle pass from private smallholdings into the Forest itself. The pond has a great deal of wildlife interest, of which the most spectacular are the white drifts of bog-bean flowers in late spring. Pike, perch, rudd, roach, bream, tench, carp and eels are all found here. (Car park; toilets; often an ice-cream van; fishing permits avail-able.)

THE VERDERERS

The Verderers' Court of Norman times had the function of protecting the 'vert' – the greenery of the Forest which provided food and cover for the king's deer. A commoner who shot a deer might be punished by the removal of a hand or even execution. Other offences included taking wood from the Forest and enclosing land without permission. Any dog which was too large to pass through the 'Crown Stirrup' had to be expeditated – partially lamed by the removal of toes, so that it was not fast enough to pursue deer.

The New Forest Act of 1877 re-constituted the Verderers' Court, which had largely lapsed by this time. Its new role was to protect the interests of the commoners. Today, the Verderers protect grazing rights and are concerned with the health of all the depastured stock. They employ the six Agisters and obtain income from marking fees paid by the commoners on their stock. The Official Verderer is appointed by the Crown; the Forestry Commission, Ministry of Agriculture, Countryside Agency and Hampshire County Council each appoint one Verderer. The other five are elected by the registered commoners.

Importantly, development control comes within the Verderers' remit. Working in close co-operation with the Forestry Commission, they are involved in most of the management decisions affecting the open forest.

A meeting of the court, officially the 'Court of Swainmote and Attachment', is opened with a cry of 'Oyez, oyez, oyez!'

Sika deer

The Japanese sika deer which live in the Forest are mostly found in **Frame Heath Inclosure**. They are descended from a small group which escaped from Beaulieu Estate about a century ago, and at the 1999 'census' there were sixty-one individuals. They may frequently be seen from footpaths through the woods, especially early or late in the day.

car park, then runs more or less straight over the heathland to Hatchet Pond, the largest accessible body of water in the New Forest.

A short distance down the B3054 Lymington road from the pond is **Beaulieu Heath car park**. This level open heathland was commandeered

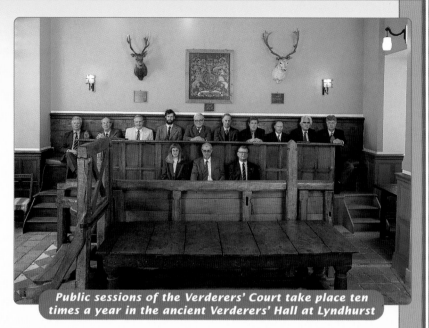

Public sessions of the Verderers' Court take place ten times a year in the ancient Verderers' Hall at Lyndhurst

from the Head Agister. Anyone with an interest in the Forest may make a presentment, perhaps something as simple as a request to enclose a small section of lawn to protect a village cricket pitch – or a far-reaching suggestion that more of the Forest roads should be fenced to reduce animal deaths. The Verderers generally give their decisions at the next open court.

Two ancient relics are preserved in the Hall. The 'Stirrup of Rufus' or 'Crown Stirrup' is of Tudor date; a replica may be seen in the New Forest Museum. An ancient oak structure which was formerly the prisoner's dock is used today as a podium for those making presentments.

for an airfield during World War II. Halifaxes and American Thunderbolts at times operated around the clock. Appropriately, a section of the old tarmac runway is set aside for enthusiasts to fly model aircraft.

Seeing Stars

A piece of advice for city dwellers: make a point of visiting the open heathland, well away from towns and villages, on a clear night. Wait till your eyes have adjusted to real darkness, then look up at the stars. The New Forest is one of the few places in southern England where the full glory of the heavens is not hidden by street lamps.

Fordingbridge & the North-West

2

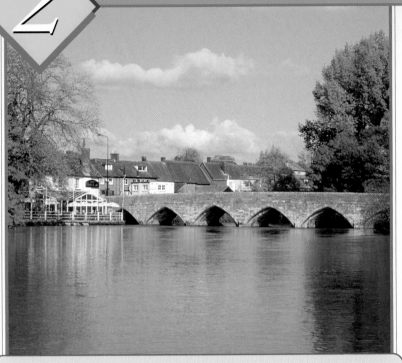

This circular route from Fordingbridge takes in much of the north-western heathlands of the Forest and some areas of woodland. Beyond the perambulation, it also includes part of the Avon Valley and some villages of the 'Western Downland'.

FORDINGBRIDGE

Although **Fordingbridge** lost its market around 200 years ago, a triangular junction of three streets is still known as the Market Place. **St Mary's Church**, at the south end of Church Street, has a fine hammer-beam-style roof in its north chapel, dating from the fifteenth century.

At the north end of Salisbury Street stands the historic **Court House** dating from early in the eighteenth century. Manorial Courts of the Manor of Burgate were held here until at least 1886. Burgate Manor House itself stands on the other side of the town's by-pass and is occupied today by the Game Conservancy Trust, which advises landowners on pheasant-rearing and the like.

The most photographed aspect of the town is the ancient seven-arch **Great Bridge**, best seen from the Recreation Ground. Standing beside the river on the north side of the bridge is a bronze statue by Sir Ivor Robert Jones. It represents the

Statue of Augustus John

As you leave Fordingbridge on the B3078, you pass the Augustus John pub – known as the Railway Hotel until the nearby line closed in 1963. One mile (1.5km) past the pub, take a road to the right, signposted Rockbourne.

WESTERN DOWNLAND

Shortly before you reach the village, **Rockbourne Roman Villa** may be visited. It was excavated in the 1950s by a local enthusiast, A T Morley Hewitt; over fifty rooms were discovered. Today, low walls reveal the layout of the site and there are small mosaics and a hypocaust. The excellent museum displays some of the objects found in the excavation and shows many aspects of life in a Romano-British villa of the second to fourth centuries.

It is well worth continuing a short distance along the same road to visit

painter Augustus John, of bohemian reputation, who had his studio near Fordingbridge from 1928 till his death in 1961.

ROCKBOURNE ROMAN VILLA

Rockbourne, near Fordingbridge (off B3078)

Remains of large Villa; museum of Roman life; full wheelchair access. Open; daily 10.30am-6pm July-August; 12noon-6pm Mon-Fri, 10.30am-6pm Sat-Sun, Apr-June and September.
☎ 01725 518541

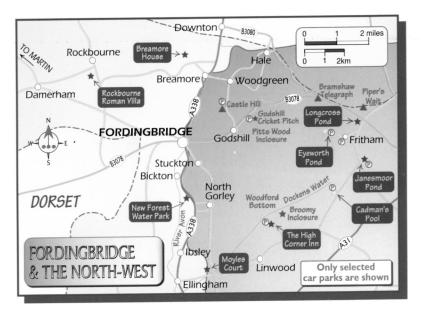

the village of **Rockbourne**, which many consider one of Hampshire's prettiest. Thatched cottages line both sides of the village street, with a clear chalk stream running along one side.

A longer detour may be made, using minor roads via Damerham, to another interesting and once very remote village. **Martin**, then part of Wiltshire, featured in W H Hudson's *'A Shepherd's Life'*. The extensive open grasslands of the chalk downs, once grazed by vast numbers of sheep, are now mostly arable fields. An impression of the former appearance of this countryside may be gained by a visit to **Martin Down National Nature Reserve**. It is a habitat for a great variety of wild flowers and many different species of butterflies and birds.

BREAMORE AND WOODGREEN

Breamore may be reached from Rockbourne along narrow lanes, or by returning to Fordingbridge and taking the Salisbury road north-wards. **Breamore House**, less than 1 mile (1.5km) from the main road, is a fine Elizabethan manor house. Built in the 1580s, it passed into the hands of the Hulse family in 1748 and has been their family home ever since.

A guided tour through the main rooms of Breamore House reveals fine examples of period furniture, including a 400-year-old Jacobean bed. A collection of interesting works of art includes *The Boy with the Bat*, which may be the earliest representation of a cricketer. There is also, rather surprisingly, a gallery of Mexican ethnological paintings. A

BREAMORE HOUSE AND COUNTRYSIDE MUSEUM

Breamore, near Fordingbridge (signed off A338)
Conducted tours of house; museum of country life; tea-room and gift shop. Open: every day in August; Tuesday-Sunday and holidays in May, June, July and September; Tuesday, Wednesday, Sunday and Easter Holiday in April. Tea-room from 12 noon; museum 1-5.30pm; house 2-5.30pm. ☎ 01725 512468

portrait of Christian Dodington, the wife of a former owner, is said to carry a curse – anyone who moves it out of its position in the Grand Hall will meet a sudden death soon afterwards!

The **Countryside Museum**, situated in the former walled garden of the house, has much to fascinate visitors of all ages – old farm tools and machinery, the reconstructed interior of a farm-worker's cottage, a schoolroom, shops and various tradesmen's workshops. Nearby is Breamore's **Parish Church of St Mary**, considered a very fine example of Saxon architecture and believed to be at least 1,000 years old.

It is worthwhile spending some time in **Breamore** itself. (The author admits bias, having been brought up

here!) The village has an extensive area of open grazing land, available to villagers, and many thatched cottages. Almost uniquely, there is no modern development, the village being designated a Conservation Area.

Just to the south of the Bat and Ball Hotel (with an inn sign inspired by *The Boy with the Bat*), a lane leads past Breamore Mill to the village of Woodgreen. **Woodgreen Common** is an attractive spot, with thatched cottages overlooking a Forest lawn with a cricket pitch.

However, the village's most interesting feature is **Woodgreen Village Hall**. Much of the interior surface of its walls is covered with murals painted in 1931 by two art students, both of whom became eminent men in later life. The scenes show aspects

The parish church of St Mary's, Breamore

of village life and all of the people illustrated – Morris dancers, Sunday School pupils, apple-pickers, poachers, cricketers and so on – were local inhabitants at the time.

About 2½ miles (4km) north-east of Woodgreen (a possible detour around narrow twisting lanes) is the village of Hale, where picturesque thatched cottages adjoin **Hatchet Green**.

WOODGREEN VILLAGE HALL

Woodgreen, near Fordingbridge
Murals of village life in the 1930s. Open: only by prior appointment.
☎ 01725 512288

A minor road, starting just to the south of the Horse and Groom pub, leads out of Woodgreen towards Godshill. A short distance up the hill, an even more minor lane to the right leads to **Castle Hill**, which gains its name from a small Iron Age hill-fort at the far end of the ridge. The parking spaces here provide a superb view of the Avon valley (see page 45).

The Woodgreen to Godshill lane passes between two inclosures, in either of which a pleasant woodland stroll may be enjoyed. Then the road descends into a valley and passes through a ford, generally dry but occasionally impassable after a downpour, before reaching the B3078 and the open Forest by the Fighting Cocks pub.

GODSHILL TO FRITHAM

Soon after turning left towards Cadnam there is a car park by **Godshill cricket pitch**. This is a good spot to set out for a walk to Ditchend Bottom, Pitts Wood Inclosure and the woods and heathlands beyond. The gravel track starting from the next car park, Ashley Walk, leads onto a ridge where the dam-buster bombs were secretly tested in World War II.

The B3078 follows a heathland ridge to the road junction known as

Bramshaw Telegraph. This is the second highest point in the Forest, 419ft (127m) above sea level. (Piper's Wait, less than a mile away, is 420ft (128m).) In the nineteenth century, signals were passed from the Admiralty to Plymouth by a chain of semaphore signalling stations. It was said that a time signal could reach Plymouth from London in forty-five seconds. No trace remains, except in the name.

After $1^1/_2$ miles (2.5km), there is a right turning to Fritham. On the nearby heathland is **Longcross Pond**, a favourite 'shading' spot for cattle and ponies. **Fritham** village has a patchwork of small fields, arranged in an almost radial pattern around the cottages, reminiscent of medieval village layout. Many of the inhabitants exercise their common rights.

Healing spring

A lane leads through the village, past the Royal Oak public house and down a hill to **Eyeworth Pond**. Near the point where a stream flows into the small lake, the ground is stained orange from the Chalybeate Spring. This is due to the iron contained in the water, which was considered to have healing properties. Eyeworth is an idyllically peaceful spot today, with ducks and water-lilies on the lake, but it was not always so (see box below).

POOLS AND STREAMS

From Eyeworth, return through Fritham village and take the road south towards Stoney Cross. The first car park on the left is near **Janesmoor Pond**. Fishing here is limited to anglers under the age of fourteen; no permit is required. Continue along the road, once part of the runway of Stoney Cross airfield (World War II), then take a right turn, signposted Linwood.

About 1 mile (1.5km) beyond this turning, there is a car park by **Cadman's Pool**. Fishing is allowed here, with permit, though in the spring many visitors come to admire newly hatched ducklings and goslings. The name of the pond commemorates Arthur Cadman, who as Deputy Surveyor of the New Forest was responsible for the creation of this pond in the 1960s. (As the

Eyeworth Pond

Eyeworth Pond was created by damming a stream in 1871. Somewhat surprisingly, its purpose was to provide power for the Schultze gunpowder factory at nearby Eyeworth Lodge, which operated from 1865 till 1923.

The product was a 'smokeless sporting powder'. One of the ingredients was fine charcoal produced from the wood of local alder trees. (Alder charcoal was also made in the Forest in World War II and used in the filters of gas masks.) Over 100 local men were employed in the factory, at wages significantly above those paid to farm labourers at the time. They walked to work from many surrounding villages and were searched for matches at the gate. On at least one occasion, in August 1871, a worker died in an explosion, a sound like the firing of artillery being heard seven miles away in Fordingbridge.

Queen holds the title Surveyor of the New Forest, the chief local official of the Forestry Commission is known as the Deputy Surveyor.)

The Linwood road continues across Ocknell Plain, turning right at a T-junction, and across Broomy Plain. About 2¹/₂ miles (4km) from Cadman's Pool, **High Corner Inn** is signposted down a gravel track to the right. The nearby High Corner car park is an excellent base for walkers to explore the valley of Docken's Water and Broomy Inclosure.

MOYLES COURT

The road then meanders through woods and heaths, through the small scattered settlement of Linwood, till it reaches a junction of minor roads near **Moyles Court**. On the lane leading north to Gorley, there is a well-known watersplash. Beside it stands an ancient tree called the 'Moyles Court Oak'. The spot is a popular family stopping place in summer,

Dame Alice Lisle

In 1685 Dame Alice Lisle, a 70-year-old widow, lived at Moyles Court. After the Battle of Sedgemoor, she innocently gave shelter to a fugitive from the Monmouth Rebellion. She was arrested for harbouring a traitor and was tried at the infamous 'Bloody Assize'. The notorious Judge Jefferies sentenced her to be burnt at the stake. Thanks to the intervention of the Bishop of Winchester, the sentence was 'commuted' to one of beheading, which was carried out on September 2nd in Winchester market-place. Alice Lisle's grave is in the parish churchyard at **Ellingham**; and a nearby public house now bears her name.

with children paddling in the stream. Moyles Court house, a fine mid-seventeenth century brick edifice, is

Both children and ponies enjoy the ford and the stream near Moyles Court

The well-known view of the Avon Valley from Castle Hill, Woodgreen

now a private school and was the scene of an historic event (see box).

AVON VALLEY

From Moyles Court, there are two routes north to return to Fordingbridge. The busy A338 runs near the River Avon, while the parallel minor road passes through the little Forest settlements of Ibsley, South Gorley, North Gorley and Stuckton. Each village has its common with grazing ponies; most were only brought within the Forest perambulation in 1964.

At **Ibsley**, the river runs adjacent to the major road. Among the thatched cottages nearby is the popular Old Beams Inn, with obvious cruck beams supporting its northern wall. A causeway leads across the flood plain of the Avon to the church at Harbridge. The meadows in the Avon valley have considerable wildlife interest and those adjacent to this causeway are the winter haunt of large numbers of Bewick's swans.

North of Ibsley, just off the A338, is the **New Forest Water Park**, where visitors have the opportunity to water-ski, jet-ski or aqua-ride on two lakes, formed when old gravel workings were returned to nature.

Hockeys Farm at North Gorley, on the minor road, is a conservation farm, with all the animals reared organically. A farm walk leads to a copse with a picnic area and bluebells and primroses in the spring; also to a deer park. Organic meat, including venison, and other produce are on sale in the farm shop – a must for anyone on a self-catering holiday!

Bickton Mill, on a loop road off the A338, just to the south of Fordingbridge, produced a widely acclaimed 'farinaceous baby food' during the nineteenth century. Most of the building is now converted to flats, but it also houses the shop of the adjacent trout farm.

Although Ringwood lies beyond the New Forest perambulation, it has always had close ties with the Forest. The tour described in this chapter also takes in the village of Burley, with its witchcraft and smuggling associations, and some of the most extensive and interesting woodlands in the Forest.

RINGWOOD

Ringwood's market charter was granted as long ago as 1226. Every Wednesday, the **Market Place** fills with tradesmen's stalls, selling everything from fruit and vegetables, through meat and fish, to underclothes and hardware. Around the restored lamp standard which commemorates Queen Victoria's Golden Jubilee in 1887, an auctioneer sells a wide assortment of objects; bundles of vegetable plants, lawn-mowers, washing machines, typewriters and rabbit hutches are among the items that may be found here.

The site of the old cattle market is now the **Furlong Shopping Centre**, with the former seed merchant's premises, Frampton's Mill, housing a café and wine bar. In the middle of the precinct is a magnificent full-size bronze sculpture of a mare and foal.

The White Hart

Ringwood's Domesday name of 'Ringvede' probably signified a ford across a river – the Avon is a short distance to the west of the town centre. In the Market Place the **Original White Hart Inn** claims to be the first inn of that name, due to a supposed connection with King Henry VII.

A 'white hart' is a stag with an unusual creamy-white coat. The variation is rare, but such stags are sighted in the Forest from time to time – seen crossing the road at night, picked out in headlights, a white stag is very striking, almost ghostly.

The original White Hart

The tale tells that Henry VII was hunting in the New Forest with his courtiers and they picked on a white hart as their quarry. It was eventually cornered somewhere near Ringwood; but soft-hearted ladies in the party persuaded the king to spare the stag's life. It was released with a gold collar round its neck. The inn where the king dined that day was renamed the White Hart.

Unfortunately, the Ringwood inn's claim to be the 'Original' White Hart is questionable; an inn of that name in Southwark is mentioned in Shakespeare's *'Henry VI'*. And the same story of the white hart and the gold collar was told by the Roman writer Pliny, concerning Alexander the Great!

After the Rebellion of 1685 and his defeat at the Battle of Sedgemoor, the Duke of Monmouth was captured near Ringwood. While imprisoned in a house in West Street, the Protestant Duke reputedly wrote to his Catholic uncle, King James II, asking for clemency, but he was later beheaded. The building which stands on the same spot today is known as **Monmouth House.**

OWLS AND SMUGGLERS

The B3347 road leads south towards Christchurch. Less than 1 mile (1.5km) from the town centre, opposite the Copper Kettle Guest House, turn left into Moortown Lane, then left again into Crow Lane, where you will find the **New Forest Owl Sanctuary.** Over 400 birds are displayed in spacious aviaries; they include birds of prey and the largest collection of owls in Europe. The hospital unit (the 'Hospitowl'!) never rejects a sick or injured bird. If appropriate, patients are returned to the wild once they have recovered. Three breeding pairs of red squirrels, the only ones on display to the public in England, are also housed here.

Every visitor should attend one or more of the frequent flying demonstrations, either in the Flying Field or in the large lecture hall, when a great deal of interesting information is given about these fascinating birds.

On leaving the Owl Sanctuary, return to Moortown Lane and continue towards Burley – about $3\frac{1}{2}$ miles (5.5km) distant. The lane crosses the Forest perambulation and heads across Vale Moor. The first of the Forest car parks on the left is **Smugglers' Road car park.** The old track known as the Smugglers' Road can be followed northwards towards Picket Post, along a ridge with views that include the hills of the Isle of Purbeck on a clear day. Unfortunately, beyond this point, much of the track parallels the A31 trunk road and the peace of the Forest is destroyed by traffic noise.

NEW FOREST OWL SANCTUARY

Crow Lane, near Ringwood
Owl, hawk and eagle aviaries; several flying displays every day; bird hospital units; picnic area, shop and café; full disabled access. Open: daily 10am-5pm March-November; 10am-4pm December-February, weekends and Christmas holidays only.
☎ 01425 476487

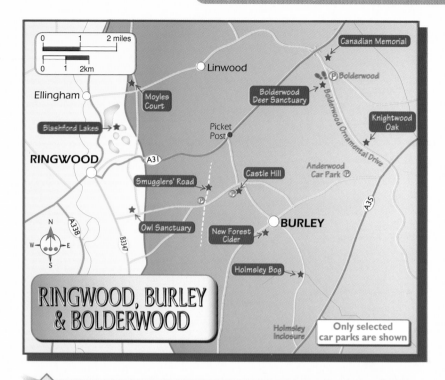

Smuggling

Smuggling was a major occupation in the New Forest in the seventeenth and eighteenth centuries. Taxes, especially on goods like tobacco, tea and brandy, were so high that 'free trading' was practised by many otherwise respectable citizens, including even clergymen. Chewton Bunny, a narrow wooded valley running down to the sea between Highcliffe and Barton-on-Sea, was a very popular place for landing contraband. Burley was conveniently on the route inland from this spot. The Queen's Head at Burley was one of many places in and around the Forest used for temporary storage of the goods before they were taken on to Salisbury, Winchester or Southampton.

It is hardly surprising that farm labourers were prepared to risk capture by the excise men for transporting illicit goods by wagon or pack-horse – a labourer's wages were around eight shillings a week, whereas one night's smuggling could earn ten shillings.

Women also had a role to play. The story is told of 'Lovey' Warne who lived near Burley with her smuggler brothers. If the customs men were around, she would stand on a prominent hill wearing a bright red cape as a warning to the smugglers to lie low. But this was not enough excitement for her. At a time when ladies only ever rode side-saddle, she would tuck up her skirts and straddle her pony, with a keg of brandy on either side of the saddle.

A little further on from Smugglers Road, there is an Iron Age hill-fort known as **Castle Hill,** just to the right of the road, with fine views from its ramparts. Continue through Burley Street to the main part of the village.

BURLEY, HOME OF A WHITE WITCH

Of all New Forest villages, **Burley** is the one that has most enthusiastically adapted itself to the needs of visitors. At peak times, when the coach park is full, the tiny village centre swarms with people. Ponies and donkeys wander the streets and car park. Donkeys have been seen to block coach doorways in the hope that a passenger will pass out another mint-with-a-hole! – but visitors should never feed the Forest animals.

Tea-rooms and souvenir shops abound, several of the latter having a witchcraft theme. The explanation for this goes back only to the 1950s,

when a well-known witch lived in Burley.

Sybil Leek was high priestess of a New Forest coven of 'white witches'. She was a familiar figure in the village, dressed in a long black coat with Mr Hotfoot Jackson, her pet jackdaw, perched on her shoulder.

She was famous for her healing herbal potions, and from her regular appearances on local television, reporting on the traditions of the New Forest. So many visitors came to Burley to try to meet her that she emigrated to the USA. Her former home is now the shop known as 'Coven of Witches'.

Among the present-day attractions of Burley are the **Wagonette Rides,** which enable visitors to see something of the Forest at the pace of a good-tempered carthorse. Another way of exploring at a slower pace than the car is provided by **Burley Cycle Hire.** Fresh produce is always on sale at **Burley Fruit Farm,** adja-

The Coven of Witches, Burley, former home of the white witch, Sybil Leek

BURLEY WAGONETTE RIDES

From Queen's Head car park, Burley
Horse-drawn wagon rides lasting from 20 minutes upwards, booking advisable at busy times.
Open: from 11am Easter-October; not in wet weather.
☎ 07000 924667

cent to the main car park. Tractor-and-trailer rides are often run from the farm kiosk, with a guaranteed sighting of a small herd of red deer which live within a large fenced paddock.

Among the common rights attached to the premises of the **Queen's Head** pub is the Right of Turbary. Turf cut in the Forest was formerly burned in the open hearth of the pub, with bacon curing in the peaty smoke above.

The hunt

The Queen's Head has long had an association with the hunt. Many 'sporting trophies' are displayed inside, while hounds and huntsmen often meet outside. Hunting with hounds has become a very controversial topic in recent years, with strong political pressure at a national level for a total ban. The New Forest Buckhounds were wound up in 1997. At the time of writing the New Forest Foxhounds still meet regularly, a fact that meets with the approval of many Forest dwellers who see it as part of a centuries-old way of life.

HOME-MADE CIDER

A little way from the village centre are the farm-yard premises of **New Forest Cider**. Cider-making was once a regular autumn occupation for many commoners, and the practice has been revived here. There is an ancient hand-operated ratchet press on display, but today's bulk production uses a modern hydraulic press.

Preparing the layers of apples, wrapped in cloths and sandwiched between slatted wooden trays, ready

NEW FOREST CIDER

Pound Lane, Burley

Forest holding with Commoners' Rights, practising traditional cider-making; farm animals for children to see; local preserves and crafts in shop. Open for sale of cider at most times, including evenings and weekends; cider pressing may often be seen in progress 8am-1pm and 2-6pm in October, November and early December.

☎ 01425 403589

Apple juice oozing out of the press

to transfer to the press, is still a labour intensive process. As the layers are compressed, the apple juice streams out. No water or other additives are used, just yeast to start the fermentation.

To continue the circuit by the most direct route, leave Burley on the Lyndhurst road. About 3 miles (4.75km) from Burley, **Anderwood car park and picnic place** has toilets and a bookable barbecue area. The adjacent woodland includes many areas of young trees as, like several other parts of the Forest, this in-closure suffered considerable damage in the 'hurricane' of October 1987 and the almost equally devastating storm of January 1990. After another mile (1.5km), the A35 is reached; after less than half a mile (0.8km) on this road, turn left into Bolderwood Ornamental Drive.

As an alternative route to Bolder-wood, take the Brockenhurst road out of the village, past the cricket pitch on the left. After a golf course on the right, take a minor road to the right and go a short distance downhill across Goatspen Plain. The OS Outdoor Leisure map gives one of the most intriguing of New Forest place-names here –'Anthony's Bee Bottom' – one whose origin is unfortunately lost in the mists of time.

BOGS AND INCLOSURES

In the valley here, the road traverses Holmsley Passage, a causeway across **Holmsley Bog.** This is one of the largest and most biologically diverse of the New Forest mires, where over one hundred different species of plants are known to grow. Mires are treacherous places, for stock as well as for walkers, and are vulnerable to disturbance, so should be appreciated only from passages such as this.

Just beyond the passage there is an isolated building, which was a level-crossing keeper's dwelling on the former Southampton and Dorchester Railway – nicknamed

'Castleman's Corkscrew'. Castleman was the designer of the line which was one of the longest single-track lines in the country when opened in 1847. The epithet 'corkscrew' referred to the somewhat roundabout route which the track followed. (The former **Holmsley Station** is now a tea-room where the Burley-Brockenhurst road, part of which follows the old railway line, passes under the A35.)

The road continues uphill beyond the former railway crossing and into **Holmsley Inclosure**. This is a pleasant place for a walk; there are both conifers and broad-leaved trees and consequently a variety of woodland birds. On leaving the inclosure, turn left onto the A35 Christchurch-Lyndhurst road; after 6 miles (10km), turn left into the **Bolderwood Ornamental Drive.**

BOLDERWOOD

The Drive is a narrow unfenced road, a scenic route with ample opportunities to leave the car and to explore the magnificent adjacent woodlands on foot.

Only a short distance from the A35, the **Knightwood Oak** should be visited. This great pollarded oak is one of the oldest and largest trees in the Forest, believed to be around 500 years old. The picket fencing around it encloses the **Monarchs' Grove**. Eighteen oak trees were planted here in April 1979, one for each of the monarchs (listed on a plaque) known to have visited the New Forest since the time of William the Conqueror.

When the Queen and the Duke of Edinburgh came to the Forest for the Ninth Centenary celebrations in 1979, each planted a tree, not far

Pollarded trees

In the past, many of the oak and beech trees in the Forest were pollarded. The word comes from the French 'poil' meaning to behead. A tree would be cut off at around 6-9ft (2-3m) from the ground and the leafy branches would be left for deer to browse. Later, the wood could be used as fuel. Over the years, the tree would grow again, but with a number of main branches where there was previously one trunk (picture page 97). The disadvantage was that it reduced the useful timber which was produced, especially for ship-building, so the practice was banned by parliament in 1698. Thus the many obviously pollarded trees in the Forest today are presumably all over 300 years old.

from the Knightwood Oak. So far, the **Duke's Tree** is growing rather larger than the **Queen's Tree**.

Both **Barrow Moor** and **Mark Ash** car parks are excellent bases for exploring the ancient woodlands with numerous fine pollarded beeches. Barrow Moor can claim to be the centre of the Forest, being the furthest point from the perambulation in any direction.

Four miles (2.5km) from the A35 is **Bolderwood car park**, one of the most popular spots in the Forest. Toilets are provided, there are picnic tables in the adjacent wood and an ice-cream van is generally parked here. An area of lawn next to the car park is much used for family ball-games, even sunbathing when the weather is suitable. Thus many of

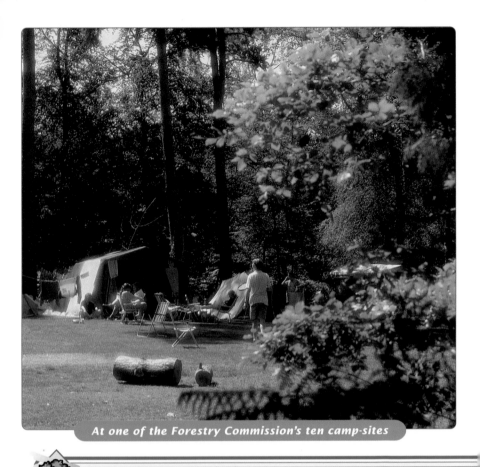

At one of the Forestry Commission's ten camp-sites

Forest trails

The **Deer Watch Trail** ($^1/_2$ mile/0.75km) takes in a viewing platform overlooking the **Bolderwood Deer Sanctuary** – take binoculars if you have them. The fallow deer which are often seen are just as wild as any of the other deer in the Forest. However, they tend to remain in these fields as the local keeper provides food for them daily, except in the autumn rutting season; so they are least likely to be seen here in October and November.

The **Jubilee Grove Trail** (1 mile/1.5km) passes the deer platforms and enters a grove planted in 1969 to commemorate the fiftieth anniversary of the founding of the Forestry Commission. Some fine trees remain from an ornamental arboretum planted around 1860.

The longest of the three routes, at 2 miles (3km), is the **Radnor Trail**, which goes deeper into the heart of the Forest and crosses the Bratley Water on two footbridges. Between a small swampy pond and the road is the **Radnor Stone**, a memorial to the seventh Earl of Radnor. For well over twenty years he was a very influential figure in the management of the Forest – a member of the Forestry Commission from 1942 till 1963, serving as Chairman for half that time, then the Official Verderer until 1966. Detailed carvings of New Forest wildlife ornament the sides of the stone.

those who park here never stray far from their cars. However, there are three way-marked forest walks starting from this car park, all on gravel paths and suitable for accompanied wheelchairs (see box below).

A short distance beyond Bolderwood car park is the **Canadian Memorial**. The Third Canadian Division was billeted in a tented camp here. For two months before the D-Day landings of 6th June 1944, open-air services for the troops were held in front of a wooden cross erected for the purpose. It remains as a memorial and wreaths are laid to commemorate those who died.

The road now traverses an area of heathland, then continues through an underpass. (It may not be clear on some maps that there is no access onto or from the A31 at this point.) Beyond Slufters Inclosure, the route joins that of the 'Fordingbridge and the North-west' circuit, through Linwood to Moyles Court.

THE 'LAKE DISTRICT'

Just to the south of Moyles Court, off the lane signposted Ringwood, is the Alice Lisle Inn. Nearby, part of the **Avon Valley Long Distance Path** gives access to the 'Ringwood lake district', an area of former gravel pits, flooded and returned to nature. (The path as a whole runs 26 miles (42km) from Salisbury to Christchurch.)

Several of the lakes constitute **Blashford Lakes Nature Reserve** which has a study centre used by schools and a hide for the use of keen bird-watchers. In winter, gadwall, goldeneye, shoveler, pochard, wigeon and other ducks gather here in large numbers, while moisture-loving wild flowers and insects such as dragonflies provide interest in the warmer months.

From Blashford, it is a short distance south on the A338 to return to Ringwood.

The Radnor Stone

BLASHFORD LAKES NATURE RESERVE

Just off the A338, 1 mile (1.6km) north of Ringwood

A collection of lakes with large numbers of migratory wildfowl in the winter months. Occasional guided walks led by warden of Study Centre. Information leaflet from Hampshire Wildlife Trust ☎ 023 8061 3636. Footpaths are open at all times; to book hide overlooking Ivy Lake ☎ 01425 472760

Beaulieu is one of the most visited places in the New Forest and this chapter features different aspects of the Beaulieu Estate. It also outlines a circuit taking in the eastern borders of the Forest and a number of interesting features on the coastline of Southampton Water and the Solent.

BEAULIEU

Beaulieu Village is picturesque, with thatched cottages and the scenic backdrop of the tidal estuary of the Beaulieu River. A group of donkeys frequently strolls down the main street, where several of the Georgian red-brick cottages are tastefully adapted as souvenir shops or tea-rooms. Beaulieu Estate, owned by the Montagu family, is the largest private estate in the Forest. But to many people, 'Beaulieu' refers not to the village or to the estate but to a major visitor attraction.

Palace House and its grounds form one of the most popular sites in the south of England, with over half a million visitors a year. It all began in 1952, when Lord Montagu opened his family home to the public, one of the first of the stately homes to welcome 'paying guests'.

Vintage and veteran

Today, a single entrance fee covers not only Palace House but also the remains of Beaulieu Abbey and the **National Motor Museum**. No motoring enthusiast will need any recommendation to visit the extensive displays of historic vehicles, ranging from the one-cylinder Knight of 1895 to Formula One cars of the 1990s.

NATIONAL MOTOR MUSEUM, PALACE HOUSE AND BEAULIEU ABBEY

Displays on aspects of motoring history including 'Wheels' dark ride; gardens; picnic areas, monorail; various rides and simulators; **Palace House** (guided tours are bookable – additional charge); **Abbey ruins**; Food Court for drinks, snacks and meals; wheelchair access to most parts. Many special events throughout the year. Open: daily 10am-6pm May-September; 10am-5pm October-April, except Christmas Day. ☎ 01590 612345 (24 hours)

Above: National Motor Museum – 1995 Mercedes and 1996 Williams-Renault Formula One cars with traction engine and a 1950s bus in the background

The Lower Drawing Room of Palace House; the arch over the Victorian fireplace was originally an open arch of the gatehouse

The Knight was probably the first petrol-driven car to travel on Britain's roads. Its maximum speed was 8mph (13kph) and its builder was fined for not having a traction engine licence or a man to walk in front of his vehicle!

Even those who are not overly fascinated by old vehicles will smile at some of the oddities, like the 1924 Daimler 'Worthington Bottle' or the 1972 Mini 'Outspan Orange'. There are other exhibits with a wide range of appeal, including a complete, and

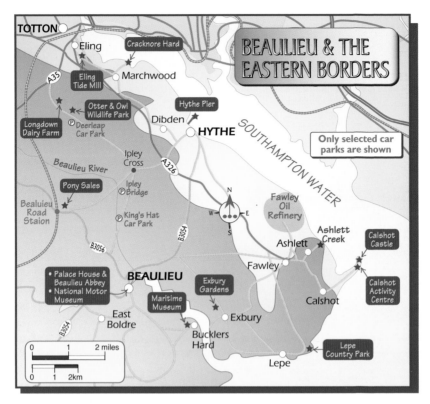

TOTTON
Eling
Cracknore Hard
Eling Tide Mill
Marchwood
A35
Hythe Pier
Otter & Owl Wildlife Park
Dibden
Longdown Dairy Farm
Deerleap Car Park
HYTHE
SOUTHAMPTON WATER
Beaulieu River
Ipley Cross
A326
Pony Sales
Ipley Bridge
Fawley Oil Refinery
Bealuieu Road Staion
King's Hat Car Park
B3054
Ashlett Creek
B3056
Ashlett
Calshot Castle
Fawley
N
W E
S
• Palace House & Beaulieu Abbey
• National Motor Museum
BEAULIEU
Exbury Gardens
Calshot
Calshot Activity Centre
Maritime Museum
East Boldre
B3054
Exbury
Bucklers Hard
Lepe Country Park
Lepe

Only selected car parks are shown

0   1   2 miles
0   1   2km

remarkably authentic, 1938 garage with all the tools and all the junk. Full-size shop windows of a similar date include Marks and Spencers, Sainsburys, Burtons and Halfords. 'Wheels' is a Disney-style dark ride, with fascinating scenes from the social history of motoring.

Beaulieu Abbey

A story concerning the foundation of **Beaulieu Abbey** relates that King John had oppressed a Cistercian community. The king then had a nightmare in which he was being beaten by monks. He decided to make amends for his previous actions by founding a new monastery at Beaulieu in 1204. It was the only religious foundation of his reign, and possessed the largest church of any Cistercian establishment in the kingdom.

The first monks came over from France, hence the spelling of Beaulieu, derived from the original Latin, 'Bellus Locus Regis', the king's beautiful place. (Despite the French origin, the correct pronunciation is 'bew-lee'.)

Most of the abbey buildings were demolished following the dissolution of the monasteries by Henry VIII. However, two have survived intact. The monks' refectory is now **Beaulieu's parish church** and is usually open to visitors; while the **Domus**, originally the living quarters of the Lay Brothers, houses an informative Exhibition of Monastic Life. The **cloister ruins**, appropriately, are one of the most tranquil spots in the Beaulieu complex.

Palace House

Palace House, as originally built, was the gatehouse of the abbey, though it has been much extended since it passed to an ancestor of Lord Montagu in 1538. Visitors can stroll through the various rooms, where members of staff dressed as a Victorian cook or housekeeper will pass on their knowledge of life 'upstairs and downstairs' in that period.

Between the house and the museum, gardens are laid out in Victorian style. An overhead monorail runs right through the museum building and gives a literal 'overview' of all the facilities. At busy times, a veteran bus transports visitors around the site. Beaulieu lives up to its claim to provide 'a truly eventful day'.

BUCKLERS HARD

Bucklers Hard, another part of the Estate, is accessible by road or by an attractive riverside walk ($2^{1}/_{2}$ miles (4km) south of Beaulieu). It was established in the eighteenth century as a ship-building community. The 'village street' was built 80ft (25m) wide so that whole oak trunks could be rolled down to the slipways on the Beaulieu River.

Bucklers Hard is a very pleasant place to visit, for a stroll down the street and alongside the river. While most of the cottages are private homes, several have been reconstructed internally with displays of life in the 1790s. There is a marked contrast between the somewhat spartan conditions in the 'labourer's cottage' and the relative comfort of the 'shipwright's cottage'.

Scenes of the New Inn are displayed in the actual rooms formerly used as an inn. Labourers, a shipwright, the landlord of the inn, a blacksmith and the Salt Officer (a collector of taxes on salt) are all represented, drinking, playing cards or doing business.

BUCKLERS HARD

South of Beaulieu
   Maritime Museum; historic eighteenth century village with reconstructed interiors; riverside walks; cafeteria; partial wheelchair access (not Museum); Master Builder's House Hotel with public bars and restaurant. Pay-and-Display car park. Open daily 10am-6pm June-September; 11am-6pm October-Febuary (closed Christmas Day); 10am-5pm March-May. 'Swiftsure' cruises operate from Easter to October, times on Pier Kiosk. ☎ 01590 616203

Adjacent to the inn is the **Maritime Museum** with a must-see model showing Bucklers Hard on Friday 3rd June 1803, three days before the launching of the thirty-six-gun *Euryalus*. She was one of three men-o'-war built here that took part in the Battle of Trafalgar. A total of fifty-one wooden warships were constructed at Bucklers Hard in the period 1698-1815, mainly using oak grown in the New Forest.

Nelson's oaks

A story tells that Nelson, concerned about the amount of timber needed to replace naval ships, gave his men acorns to plant while on shore leave. Maybe some of the 200 year-old oaks in the Forest today grew from acorns planted by sailors! Nelson could not have known that, by the time his acorns were mature trees, ships would no longer be built of wood.

At the bottom of the street, one room of the Master Builder's House is displayed as the office of Henry Adams, who was responsible for building many of the warships. From the nearby jetty, the *Swiftsure* offers regular cruises down the Beaulieu River in the summer season.

PONY SALES

Heading north from Beaulieu on the B3056 Lyndhurst road, after 1 mile (1.5km) there is a T-junction. The right turn leads directly to Ipley Cross by way of some pleasant woodland and heathland scenery, with two car parks as bases to explore this area. Alternatively, the road ahead leads to **Beaulieu Road Station**.

Beside the rail station on the London-Southampton-Bournemouth line is the Beaulieu Hotel. Across the road, between the railway and a large clump of Scots pines, is a complex of pens and platforms. On five days in the year, in April, August, September, October and November, this

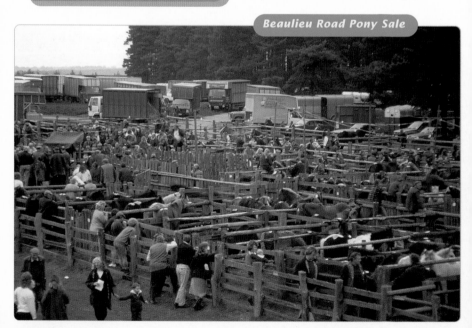

Beaulieu Road Pony Sale

deserted spot comes alive with the atmosphere of a country market. Horse-lovers flock here from miles around for the **Beaulieu Road Pony Sales**; commoners gather to see their foals auctioned; traders set up stalls selling everything a rider might need.

A short distance back towards Beaulieu, a minor road leads across an expanse of open heath to meet the alternative route at Ipley Cross. Shortly before this crossroads the road crosses a small bridge over the Beaulieu River. At this point it is a gravel-bedded stream through a narrow band of woodland.

At Ipley Cross, take the road north, which very shortly passes over a cattle grid, marking the Forest perambulation. The next $6^1/_2$ miles (10km) of the route pass by farmland and woodland which are just outside the Forest proper, though part of the Heritage Area. Just past the Bold Forester pub, the route takes a dog-leg, left and then right.

OTTERS & OWLS

A large sign indicates the **New Forest Otter, Owl and Wildlife Conservation Park**. Many of the smaller mammal species of the British countryside, like mice and hedgehogs, live indoors in re-created habitats. A 'twilight barn' is reserved for normally nocturnal creatures, so that visitors may have a chance to see them while they are active.

The various species of otters are always fascinating to watch, as they play in their large pens and pools. The enclosures for wild boar, Scottish wild cat, lynx and pine martens, as well as the large owl aviaries, are situated on meandering nature trails within mature woodland. But for many visitors, the most enthralling experience is to enter the deer glade, where sika and other species take little notice of people walking within a very short distance of them.

FRESIAN COWS AND FRIENDLY RABBITS

Only three-quarters of a mile (1km) beyond the Otter and Owl Park is **Longdown Activity Farm**. 100 Fresian cows live here – a commercial dairy herd which is milked daily in a modern computerised parlour. Longdown also houses the National Dairy Museum, with exhibits of old milking and butter-making equipment, dairy delivery vehicles and the like.

Longdown, as well as being a busy dairy farm, has many other animals for visitors to see – and for small children to feed and to pet. There are families of remarkably greedy goats, several breeds of sheep and pigs and many types of poultry. The rabbits are in walk-in pens and will happily

---

THE NEW FOREST OTTER, OWL & WILDLIFE CONSERVATION PARK

Longdown near Ashurst
(Shown on older maps as 'Butterfly Farm' or 'Nature Quest'.)
Many species of otters, owls, deer, wild boar, etc in enclosures set in 25 acres (10 hectares) of woodland; full wheelchair access; shop with wildlife related gifts; tea-room. Open daily 10am-6pm, weekends only in January and February. ☎ 023 8029 2408

LONGDOWN ACTIVITY FARM

Longdown, near Ashurst
Working dairy farm, milking viewed from gallery from 2.30pm; friendly farm animals for children to hold and feed; gift shop; refreshment kiosk; picnic and play area; disabled access most areas. Open: 10am-5pm from early Febuary to a few days before Christmas.
☎ 023 8029 3326

The rabbits at Longdown Activity Farm are very tame

take food from the hand. Staff organise regular sessions of baby chick handling and bottle-feeding of calves and of lambs, an experience which delights most children (and a lot of adults as well!).

ELING TIDE MILL

Just beyond Longdown, take care making a right turn onto the A35 dual carriageway and continue towards Southampton. At the second roundabout, turn right onto the A326 Fawley road. After half a mile (0.8km), take a left turn into the delightfully named Jacob's Gutter Lane, then left again into the village of Eling. There is a car park on the left. A short walk across a narrow bridge (with a toll to pay if you drive over it) takes you to **Eling Tide Mill**.

There has been a mill here, operated by the tide, at least since the Domesday Book. The present Georgian brick building was abandoned in the 1940s and restored in the

1980s. Today it is the only working tide mill in the world, regularly producing stone-ground wholemeal flour as well as crushed oats as feed for New Forest ponies.

At high tide, the sluice gates are closed, trapping sea-water above the mill. As the tide goes out, a considerable height differential develops between the water above and below the mill. The miller opens the gates and water flows under the mill, operating the mill-wheels. By this means, milling is possible for up to eight hours a day, although often at unsociable hours! Unlike a conventional watermill, there is no chance of a shortage of power during a period of drought.

Across the road from the mill is the **Totton and Eling Heritage**

ELING TIDE MILL

Eling Lane, Totton
Working tide mill; partial wheelchair access; displays; shop selling stone-ground flour and gifts. Open: all year 10am-4pm Wednesday-Sunday (plus Bank Holiday Mondays; not Christmas Day and Boxing Day). Milling depends on tide – phone for times.
☎ 023 8086 9575

Eling Tide Mill – the only working tide mill in the world

TOTTON & ELING HERITAGE CENTRE

122, Eling Lane, Totton
Tableaux and displays on the history of the area; temporary exhibitions; wheelchair access; café. Open: 10am-4pm Wednesday-Sunday; in winter Saturday and Sunday only. ☎ 023 8066 6339

Centre, established by the local historical society.

Back across the bridge, Eling village has a remarkably rural aspect, considering how close it is to the urban sprawl of Totton. **St Mary's Church**, though extensively restored in Victorian times, has a fine thirteenth-century chancel arch, as well as features which may remain from the original Saxon church.

South of Eling is a group of communities collectively known as 'the Waterside'. With the area's modern suburban and industrial development, it is difficult to imagine a time when the New Forest

extended to the shore here, but there are still a few thatched cottages in **Marchwood**.

There is a military port here, and a memorial near the parish church commemorates men of the Royal Fleet Auxiliary who lost their lives in the Falklands War. Follow a twisting lane to **Cracknore Hard**, where there are views of cruise ships in Southampton Docks and the workshops of the **British Military Powerboat Trust**, with opportunities for short trips on restored craft.

BRITISH MILITARY POWERBOAT TRUST

Cracknore Hard, Marchwood
Workshops restoring twentieth-century high-speed craft used by Army, Navy and RAF. Exhibition area to be developed into a larger museum complex. Short trips on Southampton Water in restored craft.
Open: weekends only, May-September; call ☎ 023 8042 8443 to confirm opening times.

HYTHE

Follow signs to **Hythe**, avoiding the busy A326. This large village has a traffic-free shopping centre with most facilities that visitors might need. Much of the dormitory development here is due to the ease of commuting to Southampton, using a route that visitors may wish to take.

A small electric train, dating from 1917 and the oldest pier train in the world (confirmed by the '*Guinness Book of Records*') carries passengers along the length of **Hythe Pier**. From this point, the **Hythe Ferry** operates a regular service to Town Quay, Southampton, with buses into the city centre. Even if not intending to spend time in Southampton, a half-hour round-trip 'mini cruise' is an excellent way of seeing the shipping in Southampton Water.

Hythe's famous sons

In the 1930s, Hythe was the embarkation point for Imperial Airways' flying-boat services to all parts of the Empire. At around the same time, T E Lawrence, better known as Lawrence of Arabia, lived in the village while he was testing power-boats built here for the RAF. Another famous resident, till his recent death, was Sir Christopher Cockerill – Hythe can claim to be the birthplace of the hovercraft.

ASHLETT CREEK

From Hythe, follow signs to Fawley. This village has given its name to the largest oil refinery in Europe and to a large oil-fired power station. But just beyond the original village of Fawley is **Ashlett Creek**, a surprisingly peaceful inlet situated between these two great industrial complexes.

The creek is overlooked by yacht club premises, formerly a tide mill, with the Jolly Sailor pub nearby. Opposite, and beyond the public hard, is the start of a footpath leading to Calshot. It follows the sea-wall alongside salt-marshes, with the power station towering overhead on the right.

CALSHOT

The B3053 leads in $1^1/_2$ miles (2.5km) to Calshot. Drive through the village to the shore, turn left and follow the promenade to the car park. Beyond this point, **Calshot Spit** is a narrow shingle headland, with **Calshot Castle** at its tip.

In 1539-40, Henry VIII feared invasion, following a treaty between Francis I and the Holy Roman Emperor, Charles V. To counteract the supposed threat, which never materialised, he had a chain of castles constructed along the south coast. Calshot Castle was built in eighteen months using masonry taken from the demolition of Beaulieu Abbey.

The castle is quite small, roughly circular, with its outer walls high on the landward side but lower where cannon commanded the entrance to Southampton Water. For the modern visitor, it is worth climbing to this position for the superb views. Inside, an exhibition illustrates the history of the castle from 1539 to the present day.

Through two world wars, Calshot was the RAF's flying-boat base. Sir Winston Churchill made his first flight from here. It was the base of the famous Supermarine S6

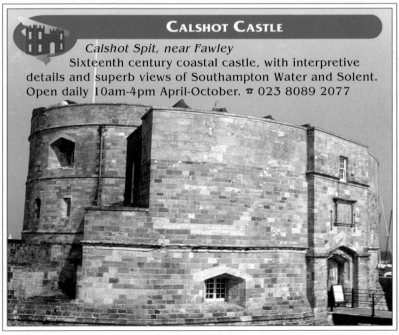

CALSHOT CASTLE

Calshot Spit, near Fawley
Sixteenth century coastal castle, with interpretive details and superb views of Southampton Water and Solent. Open daily 10am-4pm April-October. ☎ 023 8089 2077

sea-plane, forerunner of the Spitfire and the outright winner of the Schneider Trophy in 1931. Sunderland flying-boats took part in the 1948 Berlin Air Lift. The giant hangars, an historic survival of an important phase in aviation history, now house **Calshot Activity Centre**, with the S6 commemorated by a shell mosaic on a nearby wall.

Above: Lepe Beach
Right: Windsurfer at Lepe
(Isle of Wight in background)

LEPE

Head back towards Fawley on the B3053 but take the first minor road to the left, which leads to **Lepe Country Park**. A sand and shingle beach is backed by low cliffs, with views across the Solent to the Isle of Wight. With Cowes nearly opposite, there are almost invariably yachts on the water. Lepe is a popular spot for wind-surfers and, for the less active, a good place for beach-combing!

LEPE COUNTRY PARK

South of Exbury
   Three large Pay-and-Display seashore car parks; beach with dog-free and dog-welcome areas; shore walks; information centre and gift shop; licensed restaurant; refreshment kiosk; picnic areas; barbecue (bookable); children's play area; toilets (including disabled). Car parks open: 8am-9pm April-September; 8am-sunset October-March. Information centre open daily in summer, weekends only in winter. ☎ 023 8089 9108

A walk east along the shore passes a navigational beacon at Stansore Point. The Isle of Wight is less than 1 mile (1.5km) away, so gas and electricity mains and some telephone cables pass under the Solent here. Beyond the beacon, the walk skirts part of the **North Solent National Nature Reserve**. Pools in this area, some brackish and some freshwater, attract redshanks, herons, shelduck and other birds.

Near the most westerly of the car parks stand slate-clad coastguard cottages built in the 1850s. Nearby, almost on the foreshore, is the white-painted Watch House, formerly the coastguard lookout station, sited where it had a good view of the mouth of the Beaulieu River. The inter-tidal area here consists of mud-flats and attracts many wading birds such as oyster-catchers and dunlin.

EXBURY GARDENS

Leave Lepe by the lane which at first leads westwards along the shore, then head inland to Exbury; just beyond the village is the entrance to **Exbury Gardens**.

These famous gardens, extending to over 200 acres (81 hectares), were first laid out in the 1920s by Lionel de Rothschild. They are undoubtedly one of the finest woodland gardens to be seen in the country. The spring and early summer magnificence of Exbury's magnolias, azaleas, rhododendrons and camellias is recognised in the application of a higher entrance charge from mid-March to mid-June.

However, this should not be taken to imply that the gardens are not worth visiting at other times of the year. The daffodil meadow provides colour in early spring, while the changing tints of many of the trees make an autumn visit worthwhile. In high summer, the rose garden is at its best. A series of small ponds adds reflections to Exbury's beauty (see overleaf).

EXBURY GARDENS

Exbury (signed from B3054 east of Beaulieu)
Gardens specialising in rhododendrons, camellias and azaleas; picnic area; tea-room; restaurant; gift shop; plant centre; partial wheelchair access; special events through the year. Open: 10am-5.30pm, or dusk if earlier, March-Oct; 10am-4pm, weekends only, Nov, or dusk if earlier.
☎ 023 8089 1203

Requiem for a Wren

In 1942, Exbury House was taken over by the Royal Navy, and later became known as *HMS Mastodon*. In the run-up to D-Day, there were marines camped in the grounds and large numbers of Wrens were billeted in cottages in Exbury and Beaulieu. The Beaulieu River swarmed with landing craft, some too large for easy manoeuvrability in the narrow estuary. A large part of Nevil Shute's novel *'Requiem for a Wren'* is set in *HMS Mastodon* and in most respects his account is historically accurate.

Turn left on leaving the gardens and continue along this road till you reach a double junction at the Royal Oak pub; turn left and left again. The B3054 returns you to Beaulieu.

5 Bramshaw Commons & the Rufus Stone

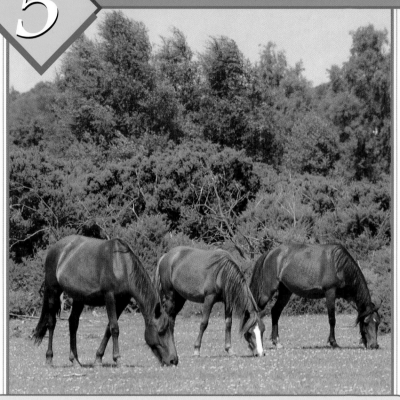

T he north-eastern part of the Forest includes several commons managed by the National Trust. Not far away, south of the village of Brook, is the Rufus Stone, believed to mark the spot where King William II was killed.

BRAMSHAW COMMONS

The **Bramshaw Commons** are distinguished on the Ordnance Survey map by the 'NT' symbol. They include seven named commons, as well as several smaller greens and most of the roadside verges around the village of Bramshaw.

Before 1964, when they were first brought within the perambulation, their position was anomalous. Villagers had grazing rights on their local commons, without charge. There were no fences, so their livestock could and did wander into the Forest proper, whose commoners pay a fee for each depastured animal. This also resulted in animal health problems.

Today the Verderers and Agisters have the same responsibilities on these 'adjacent commons' as else-

BRAMSHAW COMMONS

B3079

Plaitford Common

West Wellow Common

A36

Lord's Oak

Nomans-land

Penn Common

Canada

Blackhill

Bramshaw Wood

Furzley

Cadnam Common

Bramshaw

Stagbury Hill

Newbridge

Brook

Cadnam Green

B3078

M27

N W E S

Only selected car parks are shown

Cadnam

Rufus Stone

A31

0 1 2 miles
0 1 2km

where. The National Trust, however, is the landowner, so the Forestry Commission has no powers in the area. The commons in the west of the Forest, near Ibsley, have a similar recent history and present status.

Touring the commons

The commons may be explored on the following circular route from Cadnam, but there are several other interesting narrow lanes and byways, some of which will be mentioned in passing.

Just east of M27 junction 1 is the original 'Cadnam Roundabout', one of the earliest roundabouts in the area and an important crossroads for centuries. Nearby is the historic thatched inn, the Sir John Barleycorn. Take the A31 northward, signposted Romsey, for three-quarters of a mile (1.2km), then turn left onto a minor road signposted Newbridge. This passes under the motorway and, just after Newbridge village, enters the Forest at **Cadnam Common**.

Just after the cattle grid, Cadnam Lane leads off to the left; it is almost indistinguishable from the New Forest boundary on the OS Outdoor Leisure map. A detour down this lane leads to **Cadnam Green**, small but generally popular with grazing animals.

Continuing ahead, Furzley Road meanders over Cadnam Common, an area of short grass with gorse bushes, some marshy areas and some unfenced woodland. Just before the minor crossroads at **Furzley**, a mound on the left is known as **Stagbury Hill**. Climb to the top, where an old OS triangulation pillar stands near a Bronze Age burial mound or tumulus, for good views over the common lands.

A detour to the right at this crossroads leads, after 1 mile (1.5km), to **Blackhill**, the only car park on these commons. Elsewhere, it is usually possible to find an informal

Managing the heathland

The landscape around Blackhill is varied, with stands of Scots pine and of silver birch adjacent to the heathland. A few rhododendron bushes are very attractive in early summer. However, all three species, pine, birch and especially rhododendron, invade and ultimately take over heathland if left to their own devices. Under the partially EU-funded LIFE project, the National Trust is working to reduce this invasion.

lay-by, and the National Trust has not made its land quite so strictly 'car-free' as Forestry Commission land. Drivers should still remember that parking on grassland damages grazing and is to be avoided.

Penn Common

Returning from Blackhill to Furzley crossroad, the road to the right leads to **Penn Common**. Mixed herds of ponies, donkeys and cattle are often to be seen here, grazing on the close-cropped turf and sometimes on the dense areas of gorse bushes. Sheep may also be encountered in this area and, mainly in the autumn, pigs may be actively 'rooting' in the soft grassland, leaving small 'ploughed-up' areas behind them.

If walking on Penn Common, there are two spots where tracks lead, between enclosed fields on either side, through to the greater expanse of **Plaitford**, **West Wellow** and **Canada Commons**. This area may also be reached from the main A36 road by taking the turning signposted Canada. The unusual name seems to derive from the fact that this Forest-edge settlement was being 'newly colonised' at a time when a much greater new colony was in the news.

The road alongside Penn Common continues through farmland and A&O Woods to **Lord's Oak car park**, a good centre for exploring **Bramshaw Wood**. The mature oak and beech trees are a wonderful sight, especially in the autumn as the leaves turn colour. In the thirteenth century, some of the timber used in the construction of Salisbury Cathedral came from this wood.

NOMANSLAND & BRAMSHAW

Shortly after this car park, there is a T-junction with the B3079 road.

Furzley Common in snow, from Stagsbury Hill

The Green Dragon inn at Brook

A detour may be made here to **Nomansland** – right at the junction and then the next left. The village has the cottages on one side of the road (in Wiltshire and outside the perambulation) and the cricket pitch on a Forest lawn on the other side (in Hampshire and in the Forest). It used to be 'no-man's-land' as the Forest keepers had no jurisdiction over those who lived outside the boundary.

Back at the T-junction, continue southwards on the B3079 and through the scattered village of **Bramshaw**. Near the crossroads known as Stock's Cross, there is a small green, a favourite haunt of pigs. The road to the left leads back to Furzley; a stretch of hedge-bank here is a mass of foxgloves in the summer.

The B3079 passes Bramshaw's village post office and general store; also a small petrol station. Immediately after the junction with the B3078 and just before the Bell Inn and the Green Dragon, there is a right turn signposted 'Rufus Stone via Ford'.

However, the **Green Dragon** in **Brook** is well worth a mention. It is a thatched inn, set back a little from the road; ponies often stand around its forecourt in the summer. The interior has been extended and brought up to modern standards, but still retains some features of its days as a small commoners' 'local'. Of these, the most interesting are 'bends' of leather mounted on the wall, each with a selection of the brand marks used by commoners on their livestock.

THE RUFUS STONE

The lane to the Rufus Stone is narrow and twisting, with small hedged fields on either side. The ford is often dry, but motorists may need to drive through a few inches of water after wet weather. At the hamlet of Upper Canterton, the well-known public house, the **Sir Walter Tyrell**, looks out onto a large Forest lawn, part of Castle Malwood Walk. A short distance on through the woods is the **Rufus Stone**, with a car park opposite.

This is said to be the most visited spot in the New Forest, despite

The Rufus Stone

the fact that the 'Stone' (actually a three-sided metal pillar) can be read and admired in a very short time. However, the memorial is a reminder of the most famous of New Forest tales (see box).

If not following the itinerary in this chapter, motorists can approach the Rufus Stone from the A31. The right turn off the west-bound side involves the dangerous manoeuvre of crossing the fast east-bound carriageway and is strongly advised against. Turning left off the east-bound carriageway is, of course, no problem.

On leaving Rufus Stone, cyclists should return to Cadnam via Brook. Motorists may filter onto the A31 east-bound, turn right at M27 Junction 1, then follow the A31 a short distance back to the starting point at Cadnam.

The son of William the Conqueror, King William II was commonly known as William Rufus because of his florid complexion and red hair. On 2nd August 1100, he was hunting in the New Forest with his younger brother Henry and a group of nobles. An arrow, carelessly aimed by Sir Walter Tyrell, hit the king and killed him outright. The king was taken for burial in Winchester. His younger brother, Henry, was crowned on the 5th of the same month.

This is the full story, as far as any reasonably contemporary accounts go, but the tale has been embroidered in subsequent centuries and has acquired the status of legend. It is hardly surprising that several conspiracy theories have emerged.

Late in the day, it was said, Rufus had shot an arrow at a stag and wounded it. Tyrell shot another arrow which glanced off an oak tree before hitting the king. Fearing the consequences, he immediately fled to France, having a blacksmith reverse his horse's shoes to confuse any pursuers – there were none. The spot where he

THE DEATH OF WILLIAM RUFUS

forded the River Avon is still known as Avon Tyrell.

Henry, realising that the throne might well pass to his other brother, Duke Robert of Normandy, made indecent haste to Winchester to claim the treasury and on to Westminster to have himself crowned king. A few months later, he married Edyth, to whom Rufus had previously paid court only to be refused by her aunt, the Abbess of Romsey. As Edyth was a Scottish princess descended from the Saxon kings of England, this was a good dynastic marriage for a Norman king. Thus, Henry seems to have had motives for arranging his brother's elimination. This is supported by his later pardoning of Tyrell and allowing him to return to England.

On the day of the fateful hunt, the other two nobles in the party also abandoned the king's body. William of Breteuil left to proclaim the right of Duke Robert to the throne, while Robert Fitz Hamon departed for no apparent reason. It was left to a charcoal burner by the name of Purkiss to transport the corpse to Winchester on his cart. William was buried in the cathedral, directly under the tower. When the tower collapsed seven years later, many blamed the presence of an evil king's body beneath it.

William II, an unpopular king and something of a heretic, had always been disliked by the Church. A month before the king's death, the Abbott of Shrewsbury had preached a sermon of veiled criticism which included the words *"the arrow swift to wound is already drawn out of the quiver. Soon will the blow be struck"*. So perhaps the Church was involved in a conspiracy.

The earliest written statement of where, exactly, in the New Forest the death occurred was made over 400 years after the event. Some historians believe that a spot near Beaulieu was meant. However, a commemorative stone was erected here in Canterton Glen in 1745, because, it was said, the original oak from which the arrow had glanced, had fallen. Following damage to the stone, the present cast-iron pillar was placed over it. Yet the metal pillar is hollow – there is no actual 'Rufus stone', a final twist to this enduring mystery.

SIR WALTER TYRRELL

It is more likely that Walter Tyrell fired a crossbow while on horseback, rather than a longbow from a tree, as shown on the inn-sign

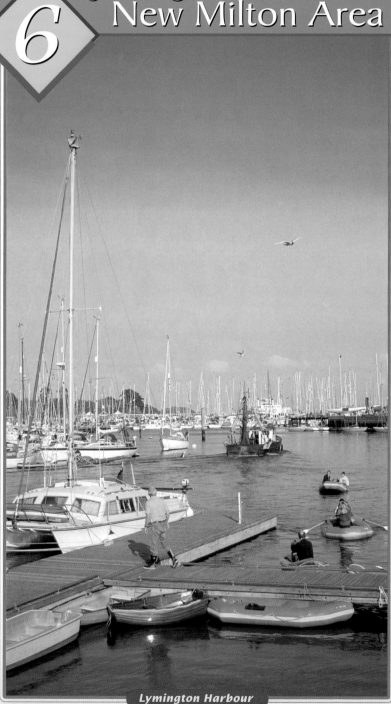

6 Lymington & New Milton Area

Lymington Harbour

The market town and ancient seaport of Lymington possesses much to recommend it to the visitor. Along the coastline to the west are the small seaside resorts of Milford-on-Sea, Barton-on-Sea and Highcliffe, as well as the town of New Milton. While none of these settlements is within the perambulation, the area has always had close links with the Forest.

LYMINGTON

The history of the area 'between the New Forest and the Solent' is very effectively displayed in the **St Barbe Museum**. It showcases the importance of the sea and of the marshes in the economy of the area over the centuries. According to Daniel Defoe in 1720, smuggling was the main commercial activity of Lymington. The production of sea-salt by evaporation was, for centuries, the most

ST BARBE MUSEUM

New Street, Lymington
Displays on history of the area between the New Forest and the Solent; temporary exhibitions; full disabled access.
Open: 10am-4pm all year Monday-Saturday (last entry 3.30pm). ☎ 01590 676969

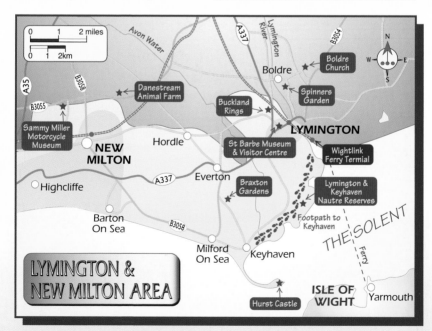

LYMINGTON & NEW MILTON AREA

important (legal) local occupation, reaching its peak of production in the 1770s. Farming, local industries including boat-building, and the beginnings of sea-bathing are all represented. The gallery houses temporary exhibitions of fine art, crafts, local history and photography.

Lymington has a long and broad High Street, running down from the imposing tower and cupola of St Thomas's Church, almost to the river. On Saturdays, traffic must defer to the market as large numbers of stalls, selling a very wide variety of goods, occupy both sides of the street.

The Quay

At the bottom of the High Street is **Quay Hill**, traffic-free, steep and cobbled. With its Georgian houses and bay windows, it is no doubt one of the most photographed street scenes in Hampshire. A short walk,

around the bend at the bottom, along the much narrower Quay Street, with tea-rooms and specialist shops, brings the visitor out onto the **Quay** itself. There is a small fishing fleet based here, with chandlers nearby for the many yachts that fill the marinas of Lymington River estuary.

Puffin Cruises offers short trips through the western Solent, with fine views of Hurst Castle and The Needles, and provides a foot passenger service to the **Isle of Wight**. The vehicle ferry to the island, operated by **Wightlink**, has a terminal on the other side of the river. There is, of course, a great deal to see on the Isle of Wight, which is the subject of another Landmark Visitors Guide.

At the far end of Bath Road from the Quay are the premises of Lymington Town Sailing Club, situated in the eighteenth-century Bath House. Alongside is a rare survival nowadays, an open-air swimming pool,

The Quay, Lymington

open May to August. A footpath starting nearby follows the sea-wall 5 miles (8km) or so to Keyhaven and continues along the shingle spit to Hurst Castle.

SEA ASTER & BRENT GEESE

The coastline from the mouth of the Lymington River to the spit forms part of the **Lymington and Keyhaven Nature Reserves**. The area inside the sea-wall is used as grazing land, while on the seaward side there are tidal salt-marshes and mud-flats. It is here that salt water was once allowed to settle in lagoons called salterns for initial evaporation, before being boiled to extract the salt.

The nature reserves have a great deal of biological interest, with salt-loving wild flowers such as the sea aster and golden samphire, and abundant birdlife. Over 3,000 Brent geese winter in the area and form a spectacular sight when a great flock swoops in to settle on one of the grazing marshes. Large numbers of terns and gulls, of a variety of species, nest in the reserves.

LYMINGTON AND KEYHAVEN NATURE RESERVES

Access from Keyhaven or from Normandy Lane, Lymington
View from footpath on sea-wall. Information leaflet from Hampshire Wildlife Trust. Open: at all times. ☎ 023 8061 3636

Brent Geese at Keyhaven

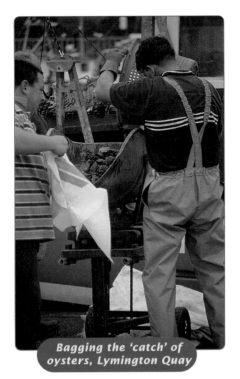

Bagging the 'catch' of oysters, Lymington Quay

If you cycle or drive from Lymington to Keyhaven, turn left onto the B3058, then left again into Lymore Lane. **Braxton Gardens** are centred around the courtyard of a Victorian farmstead, with a herb garden, a farm shop in one of the barns and formal planting in the

old walled garden. The narrow lane leads to Keyhaven; alternatively use the B3058.

HURST CASTLE

Keyhaven is a small village with a pub, a boatyard and a marina. It is another $2^{1}/_{4}$ miles (3.5km) from here to Hurst Castle, and much of this is quite hard walking on the shingle bank. There is a small amount of parking in Saltgrass Lane, the nearest point to the castle – and a favourite haunt of bird-watchers, especially in the winter months. In addition, a small ferry-boat operates between Keyhaven and the castle; a good compromise is to walk one way and take the ferry in the other direction. (The ferry also offers Solent cruises and trips to the Isle of Wight.)

Hurst Castle, like that at Calshot, originated as one of Henry VIII's chain of coastal fortresses, but it was greatly enlarged in the 1860s. Situated only three quarters of a mile (1.2km) from the nearest point on the Isle of Wight, this was an ideal spot to defend the entrance to the Solent. The castle was manned and in continuous military use from

Tudor times till World War II; guns from most periods are on display. Charles I was imprisoned here before his trial and beheading. There are two lighthouses on the spit near the castle.

To the west of Keyhaven is the small seaside resort of **Milford-on-Sea**, with a shingle beach on Christchurch Bay. A little way back from the sea, adjacent to the High Street and near the thirteenth-century parish church, is a traditional village green – scene of a pitched battle between smugglers and militia in the eighteenth century. The green is still used for Maypole Dancing and for the August Bank Holiday carnival.

MOTORBIKES & EARTHWORKS

From Milford, the B3058 leads to New Milton, but a slight detour will take in the little resort of **Barton-**on-**Sea**. The cliffs here are composed of fossil-containing sands and clays, and are constantly being eroded by landslips.

There were only fifteen cottages in Barton before 1870 – and six of these were reserved for coastguards. It is now continuous with the bustling town of **New Milton**, which also consisted of only a few cottages and a church until the railway arrived in 1888. Its most conspicuous building is a massive, castellated, red-brick water tower! The **Forest Arts Centre** in Old Milton Road stages amateur and professional theatre, music and dance, with workshops, arts and crafts and a gallery.

Leave New Milton on the B3058. At a crossroads, the B3055 leads left to the **Sammy Miller Motorcycle Museum**, housed in the former farm buildings of Bashley Manor. Extensive glass cases hold many hundreds of trophies from British

SAMMY MILLER MOTORCYCLE MUSEUM

Bashley Manor, New Milton (on B3055, signposted from A35)

One of the world's largest motorcycle museums; partial wheelchair access; tea-room; craft shops and gypsy caravan are sited in the same courtyard. Open daily 10am-4.30pm.
☎ 01425 620777

The foreground shows a 1962 Triumph 350cc model

and European championships, won by Sammy in motorcycle trials, road-racing and other events. Well over 200 gleaming motorcycles are on display, some of them going back to the early years of the twentieth century; most are in full working order.

At the same crossroads, the right turn on the B3055 leads to **Tiptoe Church**. At the church, turn right to Hordle, then left at the Three Bells pub.

Follow this lane for about 3 miles (5km) to **Buckland Rings**. There are footpaths leading to the tree-covered earthworks of this Iron Age fort which has three ramparts and two ditches enclosing an area of about 11 acres (4.5 hectares).

WOODLAND GARDEN

A 1-mile (1.6km) detour north from here leads to **Spinners Garden**, which is found down a twisting lane at

BUCKLAND RINGS

Near junction of A377 and B3054, north of Lymington
Iron Age hill-fort; permissive footpaths provided by Hampshire Countryside Service (☎ 01962 846120). Only nearby parking is provided for patrons of the Tollhouse Inn; walk back along the Hordle Road – take care, no footway for 50 yards.

Boldre, signposted from the A337. The owners bought a 3-acre (1.2-hectare) plot, already partly-wooded, in 1961. Over the next twenty years, working only in spare time at first, they gradually developed it into a sloping woodland garden.

SPINNERS GARDEN

Boldre, near Lymington (signed off A337)
Woodland garden overlooking the valley of the Lymington River; very wide range of hardy rare plants on sale in nursery; tours by appointment; no dogs. Open: 10am-5pm Tuesday-Saturday; garden only fully open mid-April to mid-September, free admission outside these dates.
☎ 01590 673347

Boldre Church

In the highest part of the garden, rhododendrons and azaleas predominate; lower down, there are boggy areas, home to royal ferns, iris and candelabra primulas. Japanese maples provide a mass of autumn colour, while a variety of bulbs flower under the trees in spring. A national collection of trilliums is maintained here.

Boldre is a scattered village in the valley of the Lymington River. **St John the Baptist Church**, reached around narrow twisting lanes, stands on a ridge some distance from most of the houses. It contains a memorial to William Gilpin, author of *Remarks on Forest Scenery*, which extolled the picturesque nature of the New Forest. When he became vicar here in 1777, Boldre was known as a lawless area, but he worked to improve the lot of the parishioners, providing a school and a poorhouse.

From Boldre, it is less than 3 miles (5km) back to the centre of Lymington.

'Through this picturesque country I have led my reader geographically; and have presented him with a great variety of beautiful scenes – woods – lawns – heaths – forest-distances and sea-coast views. I have adorned these scenes with their proper appendages, wild horses, deer and other picturesque inhabitants.'
Remarks on Forest Scenery by William Gilpin (Vicar of Boldre) 1791

While there is more than sufficient to occupy visitors' time within the immediate area of the New Forest, it is appreciated that holiday-makers may wish to take day trips to other places of interest. Having devoted most of this book to countryside matters, here we concentrate on some of the historic towns and cities and a few major attractions. Most can be reached by public transport, but the boxes give directions by road from Lyndhurst; all are within an hour's journey time by car.

ROMSEY

Romsey's main interest is in its **Abbey** church, one of the finest pieces of Norman architecture in England. The abbey was founded in about 907AD and Edyth was a novice here – the Scottish/Saxon princess who was prevented from marrying William Rufus by the Abbess (her aunt) but who then became Henry I's Queen Matilda – *see* Rufus Stone.

The present building was commenced in 1120, two years after Matilda's death, and it may be that Henry partially financed it in memory of his queen. After the Dissolution, most of the abbey was demolished, but the church was bought by the town in 1544 and has been its parish church ever since. It has many features of interest to the visitor, including the original 'sale document' with Henry VIII's seal.

Not far from the abbey is **King John's House**, a thirteenth-century stone house with a later timber-framed extension and many fascinating features, including graffiti left by Edward I's courtiers in February

1306. A linked **Heritage Centre** is newly opened.

The town has a bigger proportion of independent shops than many towns – a pleasant place to browse. The Market Place centres on a statue of Lord Palmerston, the Victorian prime minister who lived at **Broadlands House**. This is now the home of Lord Romsey, the grandson of Earl Mountbatten. A visit to the house includes a major exhibition about the life of the Earl.

Mottisfont Abbey is a National Trust property, a few miles north of Romsey. The gardens stay open late into the evening at the height of the rose season, when they are particularly spectacular.

ROMSEY
Take A337 from Lyndhurst to Junction 1 M27, leave at Junction 2, then A31 to Romsey. 11 miles (17.5km) More details from Romsey Tourist Information Centre.
☎ 01794 512987

PAULTONS PARK

Four miles (6.4km) from Romsey is **Paultons Park**, which provides interest for every member of the family. Originally it was the park of a country house, which burnt down in 1963, and the many separate rides and attractions are set in spacious park surroundings. Those of historic bent will enjoy the museum of Romany life, with life-sized displays and many colourful and genuine gypsy caravans.

For the animal-lover, there are deer and llama paddocks, 250 species of exotic birds in spacious aviaries, 40 species of wildfowl living free on the lake – and several species of dinosaurs! These full size models are brilliantly displayed in a wooded swamp and viewed from a board-walk.

For children there is the extensive Kids' Kingdom adventure play-ground for the over-fives and a Tiny Tots' Town for smaller children. The rides range from the gentle Rabbit Ride to the Raging River log flume, which is not for the faint-hearted! For those wanting a more tranquil day out, the gardens, aviaries and river walk are well separated from the livelier activities.

PAULTONS PARK

Ower, near Romsey (short distance from Exit 2 of M27) '40 attractions in one price'; exotic birds; many rides; historical exhibits; full wheelchair access; restaurants; picnic areas; mothers' room; shops. Open: daily 10am-6.30pm mid-March-October; weekends only November-Christmas; earlier closing spring, autumn and winter. ☎ 023 8081 4455 (24 hours)

Bumper boats

SOUTHAMPTON

Southampton is a major shopping centre for the whole region, but also has much historic interest. About half of the medieval walls are intact, with thirteen of the original twenty-nine towers still standing. **God's House Tower** houses an archaeological museum; the city also boasts a **Maritime Museum**, a **Hall of Aviation**, a **Medieval Merchant's House** and **Tudor House Museum.**

The magnificent landward gate of the town, the **Bargate**, still stands, as does the **Westgate**, scene of the departure of Henry V's troops before Agincourt and of the Pilgrim Fathers.

The city has many fine parks, including the extensive **Southampton Common**, site of a major balloon festival each July. Parts of the former

SOUTHAMPTON

Take A337 to Cadnam, M27 to Junction 3, M271, then Millbrook Road dual carriageway to city centre. Or take A35 via Totton to Millbrook Road. Alternatively, use the ferry from Hythe to Southampton Town Quay. 14 miles (22km) by road.
Southampton TIC
☎ 023 8022 1106.

The Bargate was the main entry into the town of Southampton in medieval times

Tudor House Museum, Southampton

MARWELL ZOO

Follow brown signs from M3 Junction 11 or M27 Junction 7

Adventure playground; childen's Encounter Village; railway and free road train; restaurant and kiosks; gift shop; full wheelchair access. Open: daily 10am-6pm in summer; 10am-4pm in winter, except Christmas Day. ☎ 01962 777407 (24 hour information line).

Siberian Tiger

Marwell. Each species has a spacious enclosure providing a habitat as similar to its natural environment as possible.

One of Marwell's success stories is the breeding of Przewalski's wild horse, a native of Mongolia, already extinct in the wild. Closer to home and behind the scenes, Marwell has been active in breeding two of the rarer species found in the New Forest, the sand lizard and the natterjack toad.

SALISBURY

The construction of **Salisbury Cathedral** was begun in 1220 and completed within thirty-eight years, though the soaring spire, the tallest in England, was added a generation or two later. The unsurpassed beauty of the building is due, in no small part, to the resulting unity of architectural style. The Chapter House houses one of the four surviving copies of Magna Carta.

1220 was also the date of the foundation of the city, which has retained its original street-plan. Many medieval buildings remain; thanks to water-courses incorporated into the planned street layout, the city avoided the extensive fire damage which devastated so many towns. Part of a present-day shop in Queen Street originated as a house built in 1306, the earliest certainly known date.

Several of the historic houses in the walled **Cathedral Close** may be visited, although most are private homes. **Mompesson House** (used in the filming of *Sense and Sensibility*) was built in 1701, a perfect example of a Queen Anne town house. **The Wardrobe**, so called as it was the bishops' clothing store, is now a regimental museum. The **Salisbury and South Wiltshire Museum** houses several displays of

SALISBURY

A337 to Cadnam, then B3079 via Bramshaw to the A36. (Or M27 to Junction 2, onto the A36.). 21 miles (33.5km). Salisbury TIC ☎ 01725 334956.

The interior of Salisbury Cathedral

national importance, including the Stonehenge gallery.

Salisbury's large **Market Place** fills with stalls every Tuesday and Saturday, with some spilling out around the ancient **Poultry Cross**. The market has operated continuously since 1361 and is only interrupted on the third Tuesday in October each year, the date of the Charter Fair. During this three-day event, the ancient houses and inns around the Market Place are incongruously dominated by the Big Wheel and other fairground attractions.

Salisbury has plenty of modern shopping facilities, both big-name stores and local specialist shops. The Playhouse theatre is widely admired, attracting a clientele from a wide area, and there are three other venues for theatre, dance, concerts and the like. The Odeon cinema is a listed building – its foyer is a restored fifteenth-century banqueting hall! The annual Salisbury Festival, generally

Midwinter sunset at Stonehenge

POOLE QUAY AND BROWNSEA ISLAND

At **Tower Park**, Poole claims to have the 'largest entertainment centre in the south', with multi-screen cinema, ten-pin bowling, indoor water park and so on. The Dolphin shopping complex is also one of the largest in the region. However, for many visitors interest centres around **The Quay**, with **Poole Pottery** being the most popular attraction in Dorset. Poole's world-famous ceramics have been made here since 1873. A tour is provided around the working pottery, while the shop has a large range of discounted seconds.

The **Waterfront Museum** contains a replica Victorian street and many other displays of life in and around Poole over the centuries. The nearby **Scaplen's Court Museum** is open to the general public only in August. Ferries leave the quay for **Brownsea Island**, a peaceful place with nature trails through the woods, the site of Baden-Powell's first-ever Boy Scout camp and a nature reserve managed by the Dorset Wildlife Trust. It is one of the few remaining strongholds of the red squirrel in England.

Poole has its own seaside on the narrow peninsula of **Sandbanks**, from which a car ferry runs across the mouth of Poole Harbour to Shell Bay, giving access to Swanage, Corfe Castle and the beauties of the Isle of Purbeck.

POOLE

As for Bourne-mouth, but stay on the A338 till it connects with the A35, follow signs to Poole Quay. 34 miles (54.5km). Poole TIC ☎ 01202 253253.

WIMBORNE MINSTER

The whole town takes its name from the **Minster church**, which dates mainly from the twelfth to fifteenth centuries. The building has an unusual 'mottled' appearance, being constructed from two types of stone, one grey and one a rich brown. On one of the two towers is the Quarter Jack, a figure dressed as a British grenadier of Napoleonic times, which strikes bells at every quarter hour. Inside the church is a remarkable Chained Library of 250 books, hardly altered since 1686.

In the streets around the Minster there are many fine Georgian town houses. The East Dorset Heritage Centre occupies the old **Market House** in the Cornmarket, now pedestrianised. **Wimborne Market**, however, has moved out of the town centre to a huge 4-acre (1.6-hectare) site, much of it under cover, and operates on Fridays, Saturdays and Sundays.

WIMBORNE MINSTER

A337 to Cadnam, then A31, 25 miles (40km) Wimborne Minster TIC ☎ 01202 886116.

PORTSMOUTH HISTORIC DOCKYARD

Visitors to the New Forest, especially those interested by the Maritime Museum at Bucklers Hard, may wish to make the trip to Portsmouth to see Nelson's flagship, *HMS Victory*, and other historic ships.

The oldest ship here is the *Mary Rose*, which sank in full view of

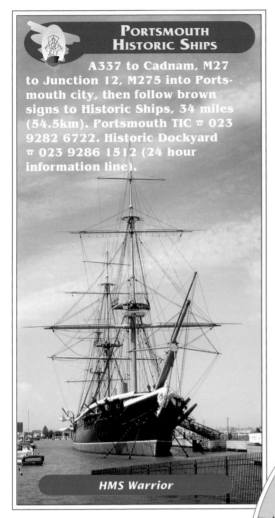

PORTSMOUTH HISTORIC SHIPS

A337 to Cadnam, M27 to Junction 12, M275 into Portsmouth city, then follow brown signs to Historic Ships, 34 miles (54.5km). Portsmouth TIC ☎ 023 9282 6722. Historic Dockyard ☎ 023 9286 1512 (24 hour information line).

HMS Warrior

his victory at the Battle of Trafalgar in 1805.

HMS Warrior was revolutionary when she was built in 1860, the first battleship to be constructed of iron rather than wood, and with steam power as well as sail. Her derelict hull was rescued and restored in the 1980s and is equipped just as she was when 700 men lived and worked on her. The captain and officers had relatively luxurious apartments, while the ordinary sailors lived in cramped conditions on the gun decks.

In addition to the three ships, the **Royal Naval Museum** and the **Dockyard Apprentice** exhibition are included in the overall admission charge to the Historic Dockyard.

Figurehead representing Admiral Lord Nelson in the Historic Dockyard

Henry VIII in 1545, with the loss of around 700 men. The remains of the ship were famously raised in 1982. Today the wreck is still undergoing conservation work and may be viewed in a special Ship Hall. Nearby the *Mary Rose* Museum tells a detailed story of life in the Tudor navy.

The *Victory* is the oldest warship in the world which is still technically in commission. Guided tours include the spot where Admiral Horatio Nelson died within hours of

GETTING THERE

By rail

The main-line from London Waterloo to Weymouth passes through the Forest. The main Forest station is Brockenhurst, with other stations at Ashurst, ($2^1/_2$ miles (4km) from Lyndhurst), Beaulieu Road, Sway and New Milton. There are also direct services to Brockenhurst from the Midlands, the North and Scotland. Cycle hire is available very near Brockenhurst station – see 'Cycling' below. A branch line connects Brockenhurst with Lymington Town and Lymington Pier stations. **National Rail Enquiries** ☎ 0845 7484950 or website http:// www.thetrainline.com

By coach

National Express runs regular services stopping at Ringwood; Lyndhurst, Brockenhurst and Lymington are served less frequently. There is a full service to and from Southampton. National information and booking service ☎ 08705 808080 or website http:// www.nationalexpress.co.uk

By car

Junction 1 of the M27 at Cadnam is 4 miles (6.4km) by the A337 from Lyndhurst. Beyond Cadnam, the M27 becomes the A31, passing through the Forest with few exit points before Ringwood. The M27 is reached from London by the M3; from Oxford, the Midlands and the North by the A34 and the M3; from Eastbourne and the South-east by the A27; and from Wales and Bristol by the A36. The A35 connects Honiton and the South-west directly with Lyndhurst.

By air

Bournemouth International Airport is 6 miles (9.5 km) from Bournemouth Central Station. Southampton International Airport is immediately adjacent to Southampton Parkway Station. Both stations are on the rail line which connects with the New Forest stations mentioned above.

By sea

P&O Ferries from Cherbourg and Le Havre to Portsmouth ☎ 0870 2424 999.

Condor Ferries from the Channel Islands and Brittany to Weymouth ☎ 01305 761551.

Brittany Ferries from Cherbourg to Poole ☎ 0870 9012 400.

A New Forest pony grazes beside a huge pollarded beech tree near Burley

Inset: Male Beautiful Demoiselle damselfly

ACCOMMODATION

Ample accommodation of all types is available in the New Forest and the surrounding area. 'The New Forest Where to Stay Guide' includes approximately 60 hotels, guest houses and inns in every price range. In addition, there are over 180 bed and breakfast establishments, including farmhouses; and more than 70 listings for self-catering. There is a **Youth Hostel** at Cottesmore House, Cott Lane, Burley ☎ 01425 403233.

Camping and caravanning

The **Forestry Commission** runs ten camping and caravan sites deep in the heart of the Forest ☎ 0131 314 6505. They range from the 700 pitches at Holmsley, with all facilities including power points for caravans, to Matley Wood with 70 pitches and minimal facilities (bring your own toilet tent!). The 'Where to Stay Guide' also lists several commercial sites of which only **Red Shoot Camping Park** near Ringwood (☎ 01425 473789) is within the perambulation.

Holiday Parks

Sandy Balls Holiday Centre (☎ 01435 653042) near Fordingbridge has won a David Bellamy Gold Conservation Award. It has also been given an 'England for Excellence' Award – as have the following, nearer the coast in the New Milton area: **Hoburne Bashley** (☎ 01425 612340) and **Shorefield Country Park** (☎ 01590 648331).

Self-catering cottages (Agencies)

New Forest Cottages	☎ 01590 679655
Hideaways	☎ 01747 828170
Bournemouth Holiday Homes	☎ 01258 858580

Specialist holidays

Country Lanes Cycling Holidays	
– supported group tours and self-guided itineraries	☎ 01425 655022
New Forest Horse Drawn Caravan Holidays	☎ 01425 477924

For detailed information on accommodation contact:

Lymington Visitor Information Centre
New Street, Lymington, SO41 9BH
☎ 01590 689000
Fax 01590 689090

Lyndhurst Visitor Information Centre
☎ 023 8029 2269
http://www.thenewforest.co.uk
e-mail: information@nfdc.gov.uk

ANNUAL EVENTS

Consult the Events leaflet from the VICs or the New Forest website. Events usually include:

- **Fordingbridge Show**, Saturday in mid-July
- **Bucklers Hard Village Festival**, Saturday in mid-July
- **New Forest and Hampshire County Show**, New Park, Brockenhurst, 3 days in late July
- **Netley Marsh Steam Engine Rally**, near Totton, weekend in late July
- **Romsey Show**, second Saturday in September
- **Carnivals** in Romsey (late July), Lymington (mid-August), Brockenhurst (late August) and Ringwood (late September).
- **Breamore House**, the **Beaulieu complex**, **Exbury** and **Broadlands** at Romsey each hold a number of special events throughout the season.
- **Paultons Park** and **Marwell Zoo** become 'Christmas wonderlands' each December.

CYCLING

Cycling is an excellent way to get to know the New Forest, covering more ground than on foot, while penetrating deep into the woodlands. At least seven organisations in the area hire out adults' and children's bikes and tandems. Most also offer tagalongs (adult/child 'tandems'), child seats, bratmobiles (towed cabins for under-fives) and even mutmobiles for dogs or cargo! Accessories, helmets and route maps are generally included without extra charge. There are also several publications available showing routes in and around the Forest.

Cyclists are permitted to use sensitively waymarked routes through the Forest. Over 100 miles (160km) of gravel tracks link the main centres by the safest and most scenic routes.

AA Bike Hire
Gosport Lane, Lyndhurst
☎ 023 8028 2249

Balmer Lawn Bike Hire
Balmer Lawn Road, Brockenhurst
☎ 01590 623133

Country Lanes Cycle Centre
Brockenhurst Railway Station
☎ 01590 622627

Forest Leisure Cycling
Motor Museum, Beaulieu
☎ 01590 611029

New Forest Cycle Experience
The Island Shop, Brockenhurst
☎ 01590 624204

Country Lanes Cycle Centre
Sandy Balls, near Fordingbridge
☎ 01425 657707

Perkins
Provost St, Fordingbridge
☎ 01425 653475

heyning   winter period when grazing is poor; formerly all domestic stock had to be removed from the Forest

inclosure   (yes, this is the correct spelling!) a fenced woodland, where stock cannot enter, originally for commercial timber production, now also managed for conservation and amenity.

lawn   an area of closely cropped grassland; the best grazing in the Forest

marl   (common right of) the right to dig clay as fertiliser or building material; no longer practised

mast   (common right of) the right to release pigs to feed in the open forest

pannage   the period of the year when the right of mast can be practised

passage   a causeway through a bog

perambulation   the traditional boundary of the Forest, last extended in 1964

pollarded   applied to a tree which had branches cut when it was young, resulting in several main branches rather than one trunk

presentment   a verbal application or statement made to the Verderers during their open court

purlieu   An area on the forest edge, historically freed from Forest Law

ride   a wide trackway through woodland

shade   an established spot where ponies and cattle regularly gather in hot weather (also used as a verb)

turbary   (common right of) the right to cut turf (peat) for fuel; no longer practised

Verderers   the ten officials who meet in open court ten times a year and whose major function is to protect the rights of the commoners

Water   (in place-names) a stream

GOLF

Barton-on-Sea Golf Club	☎ 01425 615308
Bramshaw Golf Club	☎ 023 8081 3433
Brockenhurst Manor Golf Club	☎ 01590 623332
Burley Golf Club (9 holes)	☎ 01245 402432
Dibden Golf Centre, near Hythe	☎ 023 8084 5596
Hamptworth Golf and Country Club	☎ 01794 390155
New Forest Golf Club, Lyndhurst	☎ 023 8028 2752
Paultons Golf Centre	☎ 023 8081 3345

The Montagu Arms, Beaulieu

The Ober Water in winter

GUIDED WALKS

The Forestry Commission publishes an annual '*What's On*' leaflet which lists a variety of walks and activities within the Forest run by the Rangers, from April till Christmas. These run at various times of day, and have previously included deer-watching, the dawn chorus, and 'creatures of the twilight'. There may be opportunities to visit a commercial woodland with a forester, to learn from the skills of a wildlife artist or to join a storyteller in the depths of the woods. There are small charges for most of these events, but even the free ones need to be pre-booked. Information and booking ☎ 023 8028 3141.

There are regular Guided Walks, led by professional guides registered with the Southern Tourist Board, in each of the towns and cities listed in the 'Excursions' chapter. These are highly recommended; details may be obtained from TICs.

HORSE RIDING

All the following establishments offer direct access to the Forest, for rides from one hour upwards, for both beginners and experienced riders.

Arniss Riding Stables
Godshill, near Fordingbridge
☎ 01425 654114

Bagnum Riding Centre
Near Ringwood ☎ 01425 476263

Burley Manor Riding Stables
☎ 01425 403489

Burley-Villa School of Riding
Bashley near New Milton; 'Western Riding in the New Forest'
☎ 01425 610278

Fir Tree Farm Equestrian Centre
Ogdens, near Fordingbridge
☎ 01425 654744

Ford Cottage Stables
Burley Road, Brockenhurst
☎ 01590 623043

Forest Park Riding Centre
Rhinefield Road, Brockenhurst
☎ 01590 623429

New Park Manor Stables
Near Brockenhurst
☎ 01590 623919

Silver Horseshoe Riding Centre,
Hale, near Fordingbridge
☎ 01725 510678

MAPS

The whole of the New Forest is covered by Ordnance Survey Outdoor Leisure map 22 (New Forest) at a scale of $2^{1}/_{2}$ inches to 1 mile (4cm to 1km) and this map is very highly recommended to all visitors.

In the OS Landranger ($1\frac{1}{4}$ inch to 1 mile or 2cm to 1km) series, the Forest is divided between sheets 195 (Bournemouth) and 196 (Solent and Isle of Wight).

MARKETS

Christchurch – Monday
Farmers' Markets – last Sunday in the month at Winchester (mid-month in December); occasionally also at Romsey, Ringwood and Hyde. ☎ 01962 845135 www.hants.gov.uk/farmersmarkets
Highcliffe – Friday
Hythe – Tuesday
Lymington – Saturday
Ringwood – Wednesday
Romsey – Tuesday and Friday
Salisbury – Tuesday and Saturday
Totton – Wednesday
Wimborne – Friday, Saturday, Sunday
Winchester – Wednesday, Friday and Saturday

PARKING

Parking in the main centres such as Lyndhurst and Brockenhurst is provided by the New Forest District Council and remains free after a short-lived experiment with Pay-and-Display.

The car parks sited within the open forest are provided by the Forestry Commission. The most popular ones have toilet facilities – Blackwater, Whitefield Moor, Wilverley Plain, Hatchet Pond, Reptile Centre. Anderwood and Wilverley Inclosures have **barbecue sites** (bookable ☎ 023 8028 3141). Other popular spots include Knightwood, Rufus Stone, Bolton's Bench and Balmer Lawn. There are around 110 other small car parks within the Forest – but a number have been closed recently to protect sensitive environments; they will still be found on older maps. Some car parks have advisory Pay-and-Display meters; money contributed benefits the general management of the New Forest.

PUBLIC TRANSPORT

The New Forest suffers from too many cars. Using public transport will help to reduce pollution and congestion – and enable visitors to undertake linear walks. A very frequent train service crosses the Forest and there are reasonably frequent bus services between Southampton, Lyndhurst, Brockenhurst and Lymington, as well as along the Waterside and the Avon Valley. Other villages are less frequently served, but careful use of the '*New Forest Annual Travel Guide*' will make most journeys possible. This guide contains timetables for all local train, bus, coach and ferry services.

SWIMMING POOLS & LEISURE CENTRES

Seawater Baths (open-air)
Bath Road, Lymington   ☎ 01590 674865
The Rapids of Romsey   ☎ 01794 830333
Applemore Recreation Centre
Dibden, near Hythe   ☎ 023 8084 4288
Calshot Activity Centre
Calshot Spit   ☎ 023 8089 2077
Lymington Recreation Centre
North Street, Pennington   ☎ 01590 670333
New Milton Recreation Centre
Gore Road, New Milton   ☎ 01425 617441
Ringwood Recreation Centre
(as seen in *'The Brittas Empire'*)
Parsonage Barn Lane, Ringwood   ☎ 01425 478813
Totton Recreation Centre
Water Lane, Totton   ☎ 023 8086 7474

VISITOR INFORMATION CENTRES
(VICS OR TICS)

Lyndhurst   ☎ 023 8028 2269   **Open only in the summer season:**
Lymington   ☎ 01590 672422   **Rownhams** (M27 services)
Ringwood   ☎ 01425 470896   ☎ 023 8073 0345
information@nfdc.gov.uk   **Fordingbridge**   ☎ 01425 654560

See also boxes in the 'Excursions' chapter.

WEATHER

Seven-day forecasts for Hampshire, Weathercall ☎ 09068 500 403 (premium rate).

THE FOREST BY EDWARD RUTHERFURD

Shortly before this Visitor Guide went to press, a new historical novel was published which should be of interest to all visitors to the area. Edward Rutherfurd is already well-known for his previous books *Sarum*, *Russka* and *London*. Now he has produced *The Forest*, a long novel which chronicles the history of a number of fictional families in the New Forest from the time of William Rufus through to 2000, the 900th anniversary of the king's death. Into this fiction, he weaves all of the most important historical events of each period, including the tragic case of Alice Lisle, the importance of smuggling in the area and changes in the fortunes of commoners and gentry alike.

• INDEX •

· INDEX ·

LANDMARK VISITORS GUIDES

Cornwall
ISBN: 1 84306 034 5
256pp, Full colour
£10.95

Devon
ISBN: 1 84306 003 5
192pp, Full colour
£10.95

Dorset
ISBN: 1 84306 001 9
224pp, Full colour
£10.95

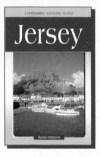

Jersey
ISBN: 1 901522 93 8
208pp, Full colour
£10.95

Shakespeare Country
ISBN: 1 84306 002 7
208pp, Full colour
£10.95

Somerset
ISBN: 1 901522 40 7
224pp, Full colour
£10.95

East Anglia
ISBN: 1 901522 58 X
224pp, Full colour
£9.95

Scotland
ISBN: 1 901522 18 0
288pp, Full colour
£11.95

Hampshire
ISBN: 1 901522 14 8
224pp, Full colour
£9.95

Guernsey
ISBN: 1 901522 48 2
224pp, Full colour
£9.95

Harrogate
ISBN: 1 901522 55 5
96pp, Full colour
£4.95

Lake District
ISBN: 1 901522 38 5
224pp, Full colour
£9.95

Peak District
ISBN: 1 901522 25 3
240pp, Full colour
£9.99

Southern Lakeland
ISBN: 1 901522 53 9
96pp, Full colour
£5.95

Southern Peak
ISBN: 1 901522 27 X
96pp, Full colour
£5.95

West Cornwall
ISBN: 1 901522 24 5
96pp, Full colour
£5.95

South Devon
ISBN: 1 901522 52 0
96pp, Full colour
£5.95

Dartmoor
ISBN: 1 901522 69 5
96pp, Full colour
£5.95

Isle of Wight
ISBN: 1 84306 053 1
112pp, Full colour
£6.50

Hereford
ISBN: 1 901522 72 5
96pp, Full colour
£5.95

Yorkshire Dales
ISBN: 1 901522 41 5
224pp, Full colour
£9.95

Pack
2 months
into
2 weeks
with your
Landmark
Visitors
Guides

Published by
Landmark Publishing Ltd,
Ashbourne Hall, Cocayne Aveune, Ashbourne, Derbyshire DE6 1EJ England
Tel: (01335) 347349 Fax: (01335) 347303
e-mail: landmark@clara.net Web site: landmarkpublishing.co.uk

ISBN 1 84306 062 0

© **Gerald Ponting 2002**

2nd Edition

British Library Cataloguing in Publication Data: a catalogue record for this
book is available from the British Library.

Print: Gutenberg Press Ltd, Malta
Cartography & design: Samantha Witham

Front cover: New Forest ponies on Swan Green
Back cover top: Exbury Gardens; **bottom:** A family picnic on a Forest lawn

Picture Credits

All photography by Gerald Ponting except:–
Brian J Woodruffe: 12, 16T, 72

Helen Charlton: 9

International Photobank: Front cover
Lindsey Porter: Back cover top, 4, 25, 31, 39B, 42,
68/9, 76, 84, 92, 95 both, 97, 103T

New Forest District Council: Back cover bottom, 27, 30, 34, 35, 58, 79T

Paultons Park: 86
Phil Green: 3, 10T, 13B, 14, 97 inset

Spinners Garden: 82

The Verderers of the New Forest: 37